Faulty Towers

Tenure and the Structure of Higher Education

T0158647

Faulty Towers

*Tenure and the Structure
of Higher Education*

Ryan C. Amacher
Roger E. Meiners

The INDEPENDENT INSTITUTE

Oakland, California

The Independent Institute
100 Swan Way, Oakland, CA 94621-1428
Telephone: 510-632-1366 • Fax: 510-568-6040
Email: info@independent.org
Website: www.independent.org

ISBN: 0-945999-89-5
Cataloging-In-Publication Data available from the Library of Congress

10 9 8 7 6 5 4 3 2 1

The INDEPENDENT INSTITUTE

THE INDEPENDENT INSTITUTE is a non-profit, non-partisan, scholarly research and educational organization that sponsors comprehensive studies of the political economy of critical social, economic, legal, and environmental issues.

The politicization of decision-making in society has too often confined public debate to the narrow reconsideration of existing policies. Given the prevailing influence of partisan interests, little social innovation has occurred. In order to understand both the nature of and possible solutions to major public issues, The Independent Institute's program adheres to the highest standards of independent inquiry and is pursued regardless of prevailing political or social biases and conventions. The resulting studies are widely distributed as books and other publications, and are publicly debated through numerous conference and media programs.

Through this uncommon independence, depth, and clarity, The Independent Institute pushes at the frontiers of our knowledge, redefines the debate over public issues, and fosters new and effective directions for government reform.

Contents

Preface

Attempts to try to understand the odd institution called higher education go back at least to the time of Adam Smith. Like Smith, but not as eloquent, we apply the lens of economics to the world we have occupied since we started as students in the 1960s. It is a project that has interested us for some time because most academics are not analytical about the world they occupy. Our experience is that even economists who are sensible in applying their craft to the rest of the world often say foolish things about the academic domain. We cannot claim pure objectivity, but we attempt to employ straightforward economic analysis in trying to understand the complex institutions called universities and the even more complex humans who occupy them.

We would like to thank a number of friends for their insightful comments and criticisms on the manuscript, including Bruce Beattie from the University of Arizona, David Boaz from the Cato Institute, Donald Boudreaux and Alex Tabarrok of George Mason University, Stephen Happel from Arizona State Univerity, the late Paul Heyne from the University of Washington, Candace de Russy from the State University of New York Board of Trustees, and Bruce Yandle from Clemson University. We owe original inspiration on this topic to Armen Alchian, Henry Manne, and the late Robert Staaf. They are not, of course, responsible for any errors of logic that remain, which we blame on each other. We also appreciate the generous financial support of the Gordon and Mary Cain Foundation, the Earhart Foundation, and the Roe Foundation.

Finally, we thank the Independent Institute for its continuing tradition of supporting original works about higher education.

Introduction

Many college graduates have warm spots in their hearts for their alma maters. For many of us, college was a halfway house between the shelter of home and the responsibilities of the working world. Most current and former college students have no more reason to be concerned with the details of the production of higher education than they do with the details of how Wal-Mart works. But just as those in retailing study the workings of Wal-Mart, those in higher education and those who are close observers of it tend to have strong opinions about it.

The problem with opinions is that, for critics especially, reason may go out the window: "Almost single-handedly, the professors—working steadily and systematically—have destroyed the university as a center of learning and have desolated higher education, which is no longer higher or much of an education" (Sykes 1988, 4). Such inflamed rhetoric has little to do with the mundane grunt work at universities. No doubt, with approximately a million college teachers in the United States, there are some loonies out there, but to focus on some individuals' personal behavior misses the larger picture.

Similarly, professors who work at universities sometimes speak as if barbarians are at the gate, threatening the survival of the ivory tower. The general secretary of the American Association of University Professors (AAUP) contends that "Ours is a profession under siege" ("AAUP at Work" 2002). A professor at Tulane bristles that "faculty members must fight to preserve academic freedom"

(Carroll 2000). Despite blusters from those who think colleges have become hotbeds of Marxist ideology and other depravities, and from those who think Joe McCarthy is lurking under their desks to haul them before the House Un-American Activities Committee, college today looks much like it did decades ago.

Indeed, we think that is a problem. Higher education is serious business, yet it has changed very little, in rhetoric or design, in decades. Almost two-thirds of all high school graduates now attend at least some college, and approximately $200 billion is spent on the enterprise each year.[1] An industry that size is important to the economy and should be expected to change—to become more efficient and competitive—as producers in other industries are expected to do so.

In arguments about the state of higher education, college faculty tend to focus on tenure because of the normal human instinct to protect what one has. Their pronouncements may be couched in terms of protecting academic freedom, but they are as concerned about keeping their jobs as employees in any occupation are. Richard Chait, a distinguished professor of education at Harvard who has studied tenure for years and who has been the center of controversy over attempts to reform tenure at some universities, notes that since the late 1990s concern about tenure has been elevated (2002, 6–26). He attributes the concern, which has produced much smoke but little fire, to increased talk about possibly limiting tenure. Tenure in higher education draws special attention because it seems a rather peculiar institution. So when the problems of higher education are discussed, tenure is often a central target. We, too, think tenure is important, but we also feel that not enough attention is given to other institutional features of our system of higher education.

As economists, we believe that individuals respond to incentives. Students, faculty, and administrators at universities are individuals, with their own peculiarities, responding to the incentives they face. Although higher education is a wonderful thing, it is, as a former college president friend of ours reminded us, just another service industry. We often lose sight of that. The focus should be on the design of the institution and on the incentives created for those who participate in it, not on tenure and not on the obnoxious behavior of blowhard professors or of those who threaten them—behavior that makes the newspapers now and then. So we discuss here many features of the structure of higher education that we believe cause problems. Because the focus is often on tenure, we begin with the origins of tenure and its current legal meaning. We then examine the roles of key players in universities—trustees, administrators, and faculty—and discuss some of the perverse incentives they face owing to the design of the institution of higher education. Then we discuss the practical aspects of managing faculty in a university before we make some suggestions for potential reforms of the managerial structure and incentives within universities.

1

The Origins of Tenure

When Harvard's first president, Henry Dunster, espoused a theological argument about infant baptism that differed from the more popular view, he had to resign from office. That was typical of the orthodoxy required of college faculty until late in the nineteenth century, by which time the churches lost their influence over many of the colleges they had established, and religious ties at state colleges were disappearing.[2] Before the twentieth century, those employed by a college were expected to follow the accepted norms of behavior of a particular religion or the views espoused by founders and benefactors. However, orthodoxy within individual colleges did not mean that competition in the market for ideas did not exist.

Many new colleges were created as alternatives to the views espoused at existing institutions. Students could attend colleges that offered widely divergent religious and nonreligious views.[3] The diversity across colleges was the bulwark of academic freedom (Brubacher and Rudy 1958, 299). Individual faculty had less freedom within particular colleges than they do now, but there may have been more diversity in the range of positions espoused across colleges a century or two ago than is the case today, when most colleges look very much alike.

The end of the nineteenth century saw the rise of what is now called academic freedom. By 1900, the presidents of Chicago, Columbia, and Harvard all asserted that no donor would be allowed to interfere with the ideas espoused by university faculty. Then as

1

now, college presidents and trustees did not care much for public pronouncements by faculty about controversial political issues, but they still defended the faculty's right to speak out. Although outlandish faculty opinions are often not good advertising for a college, especially when it is time for legislative funding, even a century ago there appears to have been little monitoring of faculty members' politics. There is, rather, a practical concern about the reputation a university could earn because of the radical statements made by some faculty members about issues outside the university.

Much is made in academic circles about cases in the past in which faculty were fired because of their political pronouncements. Fortunately, such instances were few, and restrictions on speech were not severe even by current standards. A famous controversy involved the case of Richard T. Ely of the University of Wisconsin. It is often cited as an example of how academic freedom can be infringed upon. Ely, a prominent economist, publicly advocated labor strikes and boycotts, not an acceptable view in 1894, and he was roundly criticized by the press and state legislators. The board of regents of the university issued a strong document on behalf of academic freedom, stating "We could not for a moment think of recommending the dismissal or even the criticism of a teacher even if some of his opinions should, in some quarters, be regarded as visionary" (quoted in Hofstadter and Smith 1961, 860). Ely, who did not have tenure as we know it today, was not touched.

Nevertheless, the folklore of academic freedom is that the formation of the AAUP was stimulated by attacks on Ely and on other faculty "brave" enough to weather the blows inflicted by stinging newspaper editorials and haughty speeches from legislators incensed by faculty pronouncements on political issues. As one eminent historian of higher education notes, it is interesting that although the AAUP has always made much of the nonsubstantive "persecution" of left-wing faculty members, "purges of conservative professors in certain populist institutions [never] aroused this group to similar indignation" (Metzger 1973, 139).

Little has changed in that respect over the decades.

The AAUP's "General Declaration of Principles," issued in 1915, asserts that institutions of higher learning must not have restrictions on faculty members' ideas. This document contains most of the traditional pronouncements on behalf of academic freedom (reprinted in Joughlin 1969, 155–76). It states that the role of college trustees is to raise money; they "have no moral right to bind the reason or the conscience of any professors" (Joughlin 1969, 160). It claims that people are drawn to the academic profession not because they seek financial reward, but because they are "men of high gifts and character" (Joughlin 1969, 162). Scholars must be allowed to do what they think is best; "once appointed, the scholar has professional functions to perform in which the appointing authorities have neither competency nor moral right to intervene" (Joughlin 1969, 163). Universities exist for three reasons: (1) to advance human knowledge (research), (2) to provide instruction to students (teaching), and (3) to develop experts for public service. These functions require the acceptance and enforcement "to the fullest extent [of] the principle of academic freedom" (Joughlin 1969, 165).

To protect academic quality, the AAUP founders recommended that universities take several steps. First, faculty members should be judged only by committees composed of fellow academics. Such committees would determine what questions of academic freedom were involved and whether the faculty member in question should be disciplined or dismissed. Second, such academic committees should protect college administrators and boards of trustees from unjust charges of infringements of academic freedom. Third, faculty appointments should be made only with the advice and consent of a faculty committee. When faculty are hired, their contracts should be clearly written. Full and associate professors should have tenure. Assistant professors should serve ten-year probationary terms prior to consideration for tenure and promotion. The grounds for dismissing faculty should be clearly stated, and faculty committees should be involved in such decisions.

The experience of the AAUP, the primary investigator of charges of infringements of academic freedom, indicates that violations of academic freedom are in fact unusual. In 1932, the AAUP reprinted ten years' worth of reports by its Committee on Academic Freedom and Tenure. The 1928 report was typical. Various faculty members had filed twenty-plus complaints, seeking assistance from the AAUP. "In only one case was an investigation ordered" (Committee on Academic Freedom and Tenure 1932, 341). Instances of invasions of academic freedom, from the AAUP perspective, were rare. As today, most cases alleging violations of academic freedom were brought by faculty who were denied tenure owing to poor performance or to the administration's failure to follow proper procedure, which is still the most common factor in tenure disputes.

Tenure Is Not New

Tenure as we know it today was initialized in the early 1900s, but before that time colleges did not dismiss professors willy-nilly. By 1820, Harvard had appointed professors with "indefinite" terms. Other colleges began to follow its system. As faculty ranks were created, faculty members were given the opportunity to work for advancement. However, if a faculty member was not promoted, it did not mean that he might not remain indefinitely at the college at the same rank.

During colonial times, professorial-rank faculty had a type of tenure. They were allowed to continue in office "during good behavior" (Metzger 1973, 126). During the nineteenth century, the tenure of faculty was formally a bit less secure. College charters made it clear that faculty held their positions "at the pleasure of the trustees." In practice, faculty had a reasonable expectation that their tenure would continue, but most were subject to dismissal at the will of the trustees. The courts rarely intervened in dismissals.

It was not until the twentieth century that the faculty appointment system evolved to one that requires a regular faculty member to leave a university if not promoted or tenured after a certain number of years (Metzger 1973, 122). Before tenure became formal, most faculty appointments were year to year, but it was rare for a college not to reappoint all members of the faculty. A survey of twenty-two major universities in 1910, before tenure was adopted, shows that only faculty members at the rank of instructor were reappraised annually. Those in the professorial ranks were said to hold their positions with "presumptive permanence." The rules varied for assistant professors: at approximately one-third of the colleges surveyed, such appointments were considered permanent; at most colleges, it was a multiyear appointment subject to renewal. "In all cases the meaning is the same, that the appointment is for life to the age of retirement, provided the appointee is efficient. . . . Appointments of professors and associate professors are practically permanent" (van Hise 1910, 58–59). Another professor of that period observed, "In practically all of the larger institutions professors enjoy indefinite or permanent tenure upon the first appointment" (Sanderson 1914, 892).

A Desire for Higher Standards

The AAUP was formed in 1915 by faculty in secure positions at leading universities who suffered no employment threat from the lack of formal tenure; they lived under the system of presumptive permanence. As distinguished scholars, all could easily find comparable positions at other colleges. The AAUP founders proposed that it undertake "the gradual formation of general principles respecting the tenure of the professorial office and the legitimate ground for the dismissal of professors" (Metzger 1973, 135–36). A key part of this process was the use of faculty committees to review faculty appointments, rather than leaving such decisions completely at the discretion of the higher administration.

Even before the formation of the AAUP and the acceptance of formal tenure by colleges, faculty participation in the recruitment and selection of colleagues had increased, and administrators were consulting more often with the faculty on many areas of university life. During the late 1800s and early 1900s, most large universities set up faculty-administrator committees to determine many university policies. The adoption of this practice was forced by the increasing size of universities, which made it difficult for administrators to monitor every aspect of the organization. The larger size of universities also reflected the increasing sophistication of academic disciplines, which in turn required specialization to allow knowledgeable decisions about faculty appointments and curriculum.

Trustees were passive about faculty employment decisions. By 1910, all but one of the twenty-two leading universities surveyed "reported that their governing boards simply ratified the president's nominees for faculty positions" (Metzger 1973, 142–43). The point is that before tenure as we know it was established, the faculty appointment system operated much as it does today. Trustees did not run the show. Hence, one leading academic, writing in 1918, could say that "governing boards—trustees, regents, curators, fellows, whatever their style and title—are an aimless survival from the days of clerical rule, when they were presumably of some effect in enforcing conformity to orthodox opinions and observances, among the academic staff" (Veblen [1918] 1957, 48).[4]

In 1915, the newly formed AAUP appointed the Committee of Fifteen, which recommended some tenure rules, producing the modern form of tenure, although there have been modifications. The committee recommended that tenure be granted after a ten-year probationary period, during which time the assistant professor could be dismissed. At the end of the probationary period, the faculty member would either be dismissed or tenured ("Report of the Committee" 1932, 390–91). Given the AAUP leaders' incentives at that time and the tenor of their discussion on the record, it is clear that they believed a tenure track would avoid the problems created by the prevailing "presumptive permanence" rule then in place. That is, leading scholars wanted to be sure they did not have to tolerate nonproductive colleagues imposed on them by administrators who did not know or care about quality within a given discipline. The adoption of tenure tracks was intended to *raise* the standards for faculty. "If this profession should prove itself unwilling to purge its ranks of the incompetent and the unworthy, or to prevent the freedom which it claims in the name of science from being used as a shelter for inefficiency, for superficiality, or for uncritical and intemperate partisanship, it is certain that the task will be performed by others ... who lack certain essential qualification for performing it" ("Committee Report on Academic Freedom" 1915, 34).

Colleges slowly adopted the AAUP's recommendation. A report in 1924 found that in some colleges it was still the case that "after the first year's service a man is practically a fixture unless something very unforeseen happens" (Brooks 1924, 498). At schools with tenure tracks for assistant professors, most had a two- or three-year track, not a ten-year track as had been recommended. "Reappointment, especially if made more than once, carries with it a strong presumption of permanence" (Brooks 1924, 498). A report in 1932 found that "There is a presumption of permanency for assistant professors in 91 [of 283] of the institutions studied" ("Study of Tenure of University and College Teachers" 1932, 256). By that time, approximately half of the colleges had adopted formal tenure rules, including provisions for dismissal in case of improper behavior or incompetence.

In 1940, the AAUP recommended that the probationary period be reduced to seven years, which is still the usual standard. Colleges that subscribe to AAUP standards, as most now do, must make tenure decisions before the probationary period ends, or tenure is presumed to have been granted. The AAUP does not recommend conditions under which tenure may be revoked. The 1958 "Statement on Procedural Standards in Faculty Dismissal

Proceedings" indicates that dismissal of tenured faculty "will be a rare exception, caused by individual human weakness" (given in Joughlin 1969, 41).

General Tenure Standards

Because "human weakness" is a vague standard, each college must put details in its rules about what constitutes standards for obtaining and maintaining tenure. To be tenured and promoted, one is usually reviewed on the basis of effectiveness in teaching, research (academic publications), and service (a usually irrelevant category that often includes willingness to serve on assorted college committees). Some colleges include "cooperation" or "collegiality" in their criteria, which means that the other faculty find the person to be a tolerable colleague. Nontenured faculty are largely at the mercy of their tenured colleagues, not of the administration or trustees, because tenured faculty make key recommendations about tenure approval or denial. This is a key point in the current incentive structure of colleges.

Most college faculty rules state something to the effect that to keep tenure one must maintain the standards of the profession. That is, one must continue to be a decent teacher of competent material and maintain some evidence of scholarly ability in one's areas of academic expertise. The rules are basically the same at most public and private universities. In other words, there is no legal protection for faculty who stop developing intellectually, do not meet the standards of their discipline, or become unprofessional in the classroom. This point is worth repeating: tenure does not protect faculty who become incompetent.

Trustee intervention against faculty is as rare now as it was a century ago in the days of the ranting socialist economist Richard T. Ely. During the Vietnam War, some trustees made noises about getting rid of antiwar faculty, but the court records indicate that few actions were taken. In the McCarthy era, some instances in which faculty claim to have been dismissed as political retaliation were more likely dismissals for incompetence. However, it should be stressed that some teachers in the McCarthy era were indeed dismissed because of their political views. Loyalty oaths were commonly required of all state employees until the 1950s or 1960s. Another example of legislative intervention in universities occurred in 1970 in California. The legislature passed a resolution requesting that University of California regents not allow universities to hire faculty members without a probationary period (that is, not allow full professors to be hired with tenure). The regents ignored the resolution, and nothing happened (O'Neal 1973, 180).

What Does Tenure Mean Today?

The definition of *tenure,* as designed by the AAUP in 1915, has not changed much. The most commonly used definition comes from the AAUP's "1940 Statement of Principles on Academic Freedom and Tenure":

> (a) After the expiration of a probationary period, teachers or investigators should have permanent or continuous tenure, and their service should be terminated only for adequate cause, except in case of retirement for age [largely abrogated by federal law], or under extraordinary circumstances because of financial exigencies.

In the interpretation of this principle it is understood that the following represents acceptable academic practice:

> (1) The precise terms and conditions of every appointment should be stated in writing and be in the possession of both institution and teacher before the appointment is consummated.
> (2) Beginning with appointments to the rank of full-time instructor or a higher rank, the probationary period should not exceed seven years. . . .
> (3) During the probationary period a teacher should have

the academic freedom that all other members of the faculty should have.

(4) Termination for cause of a continuous appointment ... should, if possible, be considered by both a faculty committee and the governing board of the institution. In cases where the facts are in dispute, the accused teacher should be informed before the hearing in writing of the charges against him and should have the opportunity to be heard in his own defense by all bodies that pass judgment upon his case. . . .

(5) Termination of a continuous appointment because of financial exigency should be demonstrably bona fide ("1940 Statement" 1978, 109).

The same AAUP document explains what is meant by the term *academic freedom:*

(a) The teacher is entitled to full freedom in research and in the publication of the results, subject to the adequate performance of his other academic duties. . . .

(b) The teacher is entitled to freedom in the classroom in discussing his subject, but he should be careful not to introduce into his teaching controversial matter which has no relation to his subject.

(c) The college ... teacher is a citizen, a member of a learned profession, and an officer of an educational institution. When he speaks or writes as a citizen, he should be free from institutional censorship or discipline, but his special position in the community imposes special obligations. ... [H]e should remember that the public may judge his profession and his institution by his utterances. (109)

These AAUP definitions do not indicate that professors who become incompetent in the classroom by failing to keep up on advances in their fields or by talking about their political views of the world instead of accounting or psychology should be protected for life. If colleges actually stuck to the AAUP definition of tenure, instead of to what tenure means in practice, it is unlikely that many people could find much to criticize about it.

Colleges, under the direction of trustees, establish guidelines for earning and retaining tenure (McHugh 1973, 155). As discussed later, the courts have forced universities to establish relatively formal procedures for handling the dismissal of faculty, especially those who are involved in the tenure process. Court decisions in this regard are like those in other areas of employment law: if employees have been promised certain procedural safeguards, those procedures must be followed. State employees, including college faculty, are due certain constitutional protections against political retaliation. The courts do not view tenure as a lifetime sinecure not dependent on performance. As long as a college follows its procedures properly, it is quite free to establish whatever competency standards it wishes for its faculty and to enforce those standards. Next we examine how changes in the law have impacted tenure in recent decades.

2

The Legal Meaning of Tenure

Even those who possess tenure often misunderstand its legal status. Tenure is not an absolute claim to continued employment at the same or ever-better terms. It is not the grant of a sinecure. It is not the right to do whatever one wants in the classroom. Nor, as we discuss later, does it grant greater rights to freedom of speech or expression than those possessed by nonacademics. As one commentator observed, "To most people tenure probably connotes job security. What it actually confers is the right to a specific grievance procedure.... [W]hat distinguishes the status of a tenured from that of a nontenured professor is primarily [the] right to procedural safeguards in case of termination" (Menard 1975, 256). Or, as another law commentator explained, "The heart of the tenure system is the requirement of specified cause for dismissal" ("Developments" 1967–68, 1094).

It is often asserted that tenure creates a right or a property interest in the employment position, but as the Supreme Court observed in one tenure case, a professor's claim to an entitlement in a faculty position at a public college must rest on more than his or her mere "subjective 'expectancy'" of continued employment (*Perry v. Sindermann* 1972, 603). For private institutions, the claim to particular procedural rights prior to discharge must rest on contractual relationships between colleges and their faculty. Such contractually derived rights may be written into a professor's employment contract, or the contract may incorporate, by reference, a statement of the institution's tenure policy as it appears in a faculty handbook, in published policy statements by the governing board, or in the institution's bylaws. Written statements of an institution's tenure policy are generally viewed as an implied term of faculty employment contracts even if the contracts contain no specific reference to the policy. This is true also at public universities because contractual rights to tenure are a relevant part of the employment process.

Tenure is usually granted or denied at the end of a probationary period, often seven years for new assistant professors, by a deliberate act of the governing board upon recommendation of the college faculty and administration. Some cases have found tenure by default when the school's tenure policy requires notification of termination by a certain date or establishes a presumption of tenure after a specific number of years of satisfactory service (see McKee 1980–81).

Although nontenured professors are often considered to be at-will employees, the discharge of a tenured professor without cause is breach of contract. The critical question is whether the breach is excused by one of the grounds for discharge enumerated in the university's tenure agreement or incorporated tenure policy ("Development" 1967–68, 1101; *Scheuer v. Creighton University* 1977). Court cases have also excused the breach if the professor's conduct is found to be incompatible with the performance of duties, constitutes an unwarranted disruption of the academic environment, or grossly violates university standards of expected collegial behavior (*Trotman v. Bd. of Trustees of Lincoln Univ.* 1980).

In general, professors in private institutions do not have the First or Fourteenth Amendment protections possessed by their counterparts in public institutions. Their rights are based primarily in contract. The rights of a tenured professor at a public university are somewhat broader. For such faculty, tenure may be obtained in the ways noted previously. In addition, state statute may deem faculty with a certain number of years of service or those serving in particular capacities to be tenured (*Steinberg v. Elkins* 1979). De facto tenure may be implied by a court when a faculty member has served a university for a number of years, when the custom of the school is to provide nonterminating appointments to satisfactory faculty, and when there is no explicit policy statement of the institution or no state statute explicitly rejecting tenure (McKee 1980–81).

As the Supreme Court has determined, a tenured professor discharged from a public college has been deprived of a property interest to a continuing public benefit (*Board of Regents of State Colleges v. Roth* 1972). As such, he or she must be provided adequate due process. How much process is due and what kind of process is due are somewhat dependent on the grounds for discharge.

If, for instance, the discharge is owing to financial difficulties facing the institution and the decision to discharge a particular tenured professor is based on some "objective" rule, such as seniority within the institution or abolition of an entire academic program, then only minimal process may be due (*Ferguson v. Thomas* 1970; *Johnson v. Bd. of Regents of U. Wisc. Sys.* 1974). Such minimum processes typically include the requirement that the university provide the discharged faculty with a written statement of the rationale for the decision and, in case of discharge owing to financial crises, an account of the selection process used in determining who would be terminated. The faculty member has the right to respond in writing, and the university must answer, for the record, salient criticisms contained in the faculty response (*Zimmer v. Spencer* 1973).

In cases of for-fault dismissal, added due process protections include: (1) the right to appear in person at a hearing before a decision-making body; (2) the right to examine evidence and respond to accusations; and (3) the right to have counsel, at least in an advisory role. Such rights are strongest when the case involves the discharge of a faculty from a public college, where the action will most likely damage the faculty's professional reputation and ability to acquire a similar appointment elsewhere; such cases usually involve charges of incompetence, moral turpitude, or insubordination (*Board of Regents of State Colleges v. Roth* 1972).

Specific Protections

Faculty at public universities, like other government employees, have First Amendment rights of free speech. The Supreme Court, in *Perry v. Sindermann* (1972), reaffirmed its earlier rejection of the Holmes doctrine,[5] when it noted:

> For at least a quarter-century, this Court has made clear that even though a person has no "right" to a valuable governmental benefit and even though the government may deny him the benefit for any number of reasons, there are some reasons upon which the government may not rely. It may not deny a benefit to a person on a basis that infringes his constitutionally protected interests—especially, his interest in freedom of speech. For if the government could deny a benefit to a person because of his constitutionally protected speech or associations, his exercise of those freedoms would in effect be penalized and inhibited. This would allow the government to "produce a result which (it) could not command directly." ... Such interference with constitutional rights is impermissible (at 597).

No public institution, therefore, may discharge an employee, tenured or not, for the exercise of constitutionally protected rights of freedom of expression, freedom of association, religious belief, and so forth (*Johnson v. Bd. of Regents of U. Wisc. Sys.* 1974, 240). This is not to say that the line between constitutionally protected conduct and unprotected conduct is always easy to draw. When dismissed, faculty often find it in their interest to assert First Amendment violations they had not previously pondered. Cases of insubordination can be fuzzy at the edges in this regard.

The courts look for evidence of good faith by institutions in reaching decisions to discharge tenured faculty. This review has several components. Courts generally accord great deference to an institution's determination of the bounds of permissible conduct within itself and to an institution's management of its financial affairs.[6] More constraints are imposed when tenured faculty are discharged for cause. These constraints are derived from general principles of judicial review of decision making by public agencies.

First, there should not be marked inconsistencies in an institution's determination of what is impermissible conduct when such conduct occurs. That is, rules governing appropriate conduct should be stated in a form that is not so vague as to be unintelligible and therefore subject to highly selective interpretation and enforcement. Evidence of consistency is important. Such rules need not be exhaustive; they may include other rules by reference or implication (*Adamian v. Jacobsen* 1975).

Second, the facts contained in the records should arguably justify the conclusions that the discharging authority drew from them. The authority's reasoning from the facts and from the principles applied to them should not contain glaring errors or gaps (*Garrett v. Matthews* 1979).

Third, as in all such administrative dismissals, there should not be any substantial reasons for believing that the discharging authority was motivated by animosity or bias that would cast doubt on that authority's ability to determine the material facts and to reach an impartial decision on the basis of these facts and preexisting rules (Aman and Mayton 2001, 246–53).

These factors are not exhaustive of tenured faculty's rights at public institutions. They often have added procedural rights as a result of state statutes, university regulations, or explicit contract provisions. Similarly, grounds for discharge of tenured faculty generally must be spelled out in the faculty member's employment contract, in university policies, or in state law. Courts usually must be able to find some connection between the specified ground for discharge and the professor's inability to carry out his or her duties in a manner compatible with professional standards. We now turn to a consideration of the major grounds for "for-cause" discharge of tenured faculty in both private and public institutions.

For-Cause Discharge of Tenured Professors

A 1971 survey of eighty universities specified approximately twenty-five grounds for dismissal of tenured faculty (Shaw 1971). The listing of many grounds for dismissal is consistent with the AAUP's policy of approving such limitations that are in accord with the "special aims" of an institution and are specified at the time of a faculty member's appointment and is thus consistent with case law. Although many grounds are listed at different schools, in practice the relevant list is short. As noted earlier, the often relied upon "1940 Statement of Principles on Academic Freedom and Tenure" indicates that "After the expiration of a probationary period, teachers ... should have permanent or continuous tenure, and their service should be terminated only for adequate cause."

The AAUP Statement does not define *adequate cause,* but it does make reference to incompetence, moral turpitude, and financial exigency as examples of such cause, and it outlines procedures and remedies that should be available in each of these circumstances. Similarly, the 1973 *Report of the Commission on Academic Tenure in Higher Education* expressed the categories comprising adequate cause for dismissal of tenured faculty: "[1] Incompetence (including inefficiency); [2] immorality (including dishonesty); [3] neglect of duty (such as violating institutional rules and missing classes); and [4] insubordination (including excessively disruptive behavior)" (Developments in the Law: Academic Freedom 1968, 1084). This list of causes for dismissal tends to reflect standards adopted in most university tenure regulations. Of course, terms such as *incompetence* and *neglect of duty* have more technical meaning in this statement than in their ordinary English usage.

Case Law

Before 1970, litigation by faculty who were dismissed or were not happy with some other aspect of their treatment was rare, as Table 1 shows. The table reports all cases that appear in WestLaw in the

ALLSTATES or ALLFEDS databases using the search words *tenure, faculty,* and *college* or *university.* Because many cases that appear with those key words are not on point, we briefly reviewed each case to decide if it should be included in the count as one involving a dispute between a faculty member and a university on a tenure issue. ALLSTATES provides appeals court cases from all state courts and some district court cases. Most faculty disputes historically were a matter of state contract law or were controlled by state procedures for state employees, so until federal rights were created or were "discovered" in the 1960s and 1970s, there was little reason for litigation in federal court. ALLFEDS reports all decisions of the U.S. Supreme Court and written decisions of courts of appeal. We have excluded district courts. Some of the appeal court decisions are not "published," but they can be read in the WestLaw database and so are included. The table shows a count of all cases that appear in the databases and that relate to tenure disputes.

Table 1 does not give a count of every case filed because many are dropped or settled before trial; of those that move forward, some are dismissed before trial, and, of those that go to trial, many are not appealed, so the results are not reported. The purpose of the table is to give an idea of the change in the extent of litigation. Also note that the data are skewed by the inclusion of a large number of junior (community) college cases and that the last entry of each section of the table is an extrapolation of the first three years of 2000–2005 to the full term.

Approximately half of the counted cases involve junior colleges. Most such cases are resolved easily under state law regarding tenure of junior college teachers, who are generally classified more like public K–12 teachers than university teachers and are subject to rather mechanical standards. For example, according to Alabama state law, a junior college teacher automatically has tenure after three years of teaching, if not dismissed before the end of those three years *(McLeod v. Beaty* 1997). Most cases are simple claims that tenure has been achieved; they are much like many cases filed

Table 1

Number of Reported Cases on Tenure*

ALLFEDS	Number of Tenure Cases	Number of Title VII Cases
Pre-1945	2	0
1945–65	1	0
1965–70	3	0
1970–75	27	2
1975–80	44	15
1980–85	27	18
1985–90	27	34
1990–95	20	23
1995–2000	21	39
2000–2003	12 (20[†])	25 (40[†])

ALLSTATES	Number of Tenure Cases	Number of Title VII Cases
Pre-1945	14	0
1945–65	30	0
1965–75	36	1
1975–80	70	15
1980–85	81	10
1985–90	88	14
1990–95	51	9
1995–2000	83	12
2000–2003	57 (95[†])	14 (25[†])

*dates run February to February
[†]parenthetical numbers represent five-year extrapolations of 2000–2003 data

by state employees, such as public school teachers and bus drivers, who assert that, under state regulations, they are classified as permanent after so much time in grade.

Further, the data are distorted by a relatively large number of cases from a few states, such as Ohio and Minnesota, that have peculiar laws regarding appeals of tenure disputes, which throw a larger than usual number of cases into the appeals courts. Of the remaining cases, untenured faculty at universities claimed that the failure to grant them tenure at the time of their dismissal was a Fourteenth Amendment due process violation, a contract violation, or a First Amendment rights violation. The right-side column is a list of tenure-related claims based on violation of Title VII, the portion of the Civil Rights Act of 1964 that requires nondiscrimination in employment on the basis of race, sex, religion, national origin, or age (as amended). That list also includes claims of discrimination based on disability, although such cases are rare.

What Do the Cases Tell Us?

The cases counted in Table 1 largely resulted from two changes in the law. The first and easiest to cover are Title VII cases. Passage of the Civil Rights Act of 1964 and subsequent statutes regarding discrimination in employment on the basis of pregnancy, age, and disability have spawned significant litigation in all areas of employment. Universities are no exception. Not including cases involving claims of salary discrimination based on sex, race, and age, and some involving mandatory retirement for faculty, when that was still an issue, the cases counted in the table are almost all claims that tenure was not granted or that a nontenured faculty member was not retained because of race, sex, religion, national origin, age, or disability. In a few cases, the appeals court found evidence of discrimination, but the large majority of the suits were disposed of in favor of the university so long as it had followed proper procedure. Although discrimination exists, it is not a major issue of academic freedom in the context of faculty retention.

The key issues in non–Title VII cases are claims of breach of employment contract and violation of due process and free speech rights protected by the Constitution. Most cases are brought by faculty denied tenure or nontenured faculty not rehired. In most cases where nontenured faculty are not rehired, as most are on year-by-year contracts, the faculty are viewed as at-will employees with no claim once the term of their contract expires. When faculty are denied tenure at the end of their probation period, the substantive issues are likely to come into play.

The Supreme Court spelled out these issues in companion cases in 1972. These cases illustrate well the general state of the law today. They played a role in generating the volume of litigation noted in Table 1, but, as discussed later, the concern is primarily one of proper procedure. In *Board of Regents of State Colleges v. Roth* (1972), an assistant professor of political science at Wisconsin State University, Oshkosh did not have his one-year employment contract renewed. He contended that his not being renewed was improper and a violation of his constitutional rights.

The Court brushed aside Roth's claim that his nonrenewal was improper. Justice Steward noted that he "had no tenure rights to continued employment. . . . A relatively new teacher without tenure . . . is under Wisconsin law entitled to nothing beyond his one-year appointment. . . . State law thus clearly leaves the decision whether to rehire a nontenured teacher for another year to the unfettered discretion of university officials" (*Board of Regents of State Colleges v. Roth* 1972, 566–67). Roth contended that the true reason for his nonrenewal was to punish him for making statements critical of the university administration, a violation of his free speech right. He also claimed that even if he did not have a right to renewal, he had a right to a hearing about the reason for his nonrenewal.

Whereas Justices Brennan, Douglas, and Marshall found the lack of renewal without a hearing to be a violation of Fourteenth Amendment due process rights necessary to protect free speech rights and academic freedom, the majority held otherwise: "The requirements of procedural due process apply only to the deprivation of interests encompassed by the Fourteenth Amendment's protection of liberty and property." Roth, an employee on a one-year contract, had no right because he simply was not rehired. Had he been not rehired because of a charge that he had engaged in destructive behavior, then his "standing and associations in his community" (at 573) could be harmed, and he would be accorded due process of a hearing. But, unlike some faculty dismissed in earlier years for failure to sign loyalty oaths and thereby suffered a stigma, Roth was simply not rehired. He failed to show merit to his allegation that the decision not to rehire was retaliation for his statements about political matters at the university. "It stretches the concept too far to suggest that a person is deprived of 'liberty' when he simply is not rehired in one job but remains as free as before to seek another" (at 575).

Similarly, had Roth lost a tenured position at a state university, then he would have standing to raise the Fourteenth Amendment issue of procedural protection of a property interest. He would have been due proper procedure, including a hearing, but he had no tenure, so he had no such right.

Perry v. Sindermann (1972), the companion to the *Roth* case, provided a little stronger case on behalf of the faculty member. Sindermann had worked as a teacher in the Texas state college system for ten years. In his fourth year at a junior college, where he was employed on one-year contracts, he was dismissed after a dispute with the college administration. When he was dismissed, the regents issued a press release regarding his insubordination. The Supreme Court held that his contractual basis of employment did not defeat his claim that his nonrenewal may have violated the First and Fourteenth Amendments: "[T]here is a genuine dispute as to 'whether the college refused to renew the teaching contract on an impermissible basis—as a reprisal for the exercise of constitutionally protected rights.' ... [A] teacher's public criticism of his superiors on matters of public concern may be constitutionally protected and may, therefore, be an impermissible basis for termination of his employment" (at 598).

The Court also noted that the junior college where Sindermann worked did not have formal tenure, but it did have a policy that a faculty member should "feel that he has permanent tenure as long as his teaching services are satisfactory and as long as he displays a cooperative attitude" (at 600). This policy, the Court held, "may be an unwritten 'common law' in a particular university that certain employees shall have the equivalent of tenure" (at 602). Should Sindermann show at trial such a property interest in employment, it would "not, of course, entitle him to reinstatement. But such proof would obligate college officials to grant a hearing at his request, where he could be informed of the grounds for his nonretention and challenge their sufficiency" (at 603).

These Supreme Court cases provided significant guidance in the elements needed for a distressed faculty member's cause of action, such as for improper dismissal, and apparently spawned the increase in litigation that has occurred since they were decided. However, a reading of the cases clearly indicates (see the appendix, where such cases for the past thirteen years are listed with pertinent details) that so long as proper procedure is followed and a faculty member is in fact not being fired for saying something that irritated an institutional authority, there are few legal constraints on the proper functioning of a university as a place that expects faculty to be productive, perform their duties properly, and maintain the standards of their profession.

Only a few reported suits, less than one per year by our count for 1990 to early 2003, were brought by faculty who were dismissed for incompetence or dereliction of duties. The results were mixed; if the court found that proper procedure had not been followed, the faculty member prevailed; otherwise, the dismissal was upheld. But it is extraordinarily rare for a university to be ordered to reinstate a dismissed faculty member. A small number of cases involved faculty challenging dismissal based on a claim of financial exigency by the school. Again, so long as financial difficulties were real and the dismissal was reasoned, such as closing down a department that had very few students, the courts upheld dismissal of tenured faculty.

In sum, a review of the law indicates that universities must follow proper procedure regarding contracts, as must any employer. State employers must take care not to violate certain speech rights, but universities are not significantly different than other government bureaus in this regard, except that dismissed faculty may be more likely than nonfaculty to throw in an assertion that academic freedom was violated because it has a good ring. But such an assertion does not impress the courts unless backed by substantive evidence.

States have a variety of statutory requirements regarding tenure, dismissal, procedure, and appeals for state college teachers as well as for public school teachers.[7] So long as constitutional guidelines are not crossed, states have the right to construct their own procedures. Some appear to have inflicted high procedural costs (or procedural safeguards, should one prefer to think of it that way) on themselves regarding termination of state employees. Unionized colleges have problems peculiar to collective bargaining.[8]

The question, then, is: Why does tenure appear, to many critics and even to many who hold tenure, to produce undesirable results? The idea of tenure not being granted until after a probationary period of seven years appears to be a quality-enhancing move that was an improvement on the old system of presumptive permanence. The law does not grant faculty rights to behave in an improper or unproductive manner. Because many people are dubious when we make this point, we include in the appendix an exhaustive review of every reported case in the courts for more than a decade. The point is that tenured faculty who become incompetent, fail to perform their duties, or behave in grossly improper manners can be fired. A survey of appeals court cases indicates that does not happen often. Given the hundreds of thousands of tenured faculty members, if there were many dismissals, there would likely be more cases, and such instances would be heard of more often. Ask yourself how many tenured faculty you have heard of being dismissed. We know of none. If that is the case, then the focus of discussions regarding the problems in higher education should not be on the law of tenure or on the courts, but rather on the structure of higher education. Next we discuss that structure and then some of the practical consequences of the institutional design of colleges.

3

Roots of the Structural Problems in Higher Education

Higher education is dominated by government agencies and non-profit organizations. That is, universities should be expected to be afflicted with major efficiency problems. Incentives are very different in public and non-profit institutions than in for-profit organizations. There is a greater lack of accountability in public agencies than in private companies.

Imagine a company that has no profit measure to compare performance from year to year or against competitors. The head of the organization is nominated by a committee process dominated by employees. If the employees become unhappy with the head of the organization, they can demand that he or she be fired—but employees are rarely fired.[9] In essence, that is the world of university governance. The problem is pervasive at state universities, but it exists at private universities, too.

Whether state agencies or private non-profit organizations, universities do not have the kind of financial measures that organizations in the private sector rely on to drive performance evaluations. Profit measures are key for businesses. Internal and external observers calculate the relative success of the managers of an operation by using financial measures. Colleges either operate on budgets granted by the legislature or are non-profit charities. Those that balance their budget or run a surplus are generally considered a success.

College boards and top administrators are also shy to adopt nonfinancial performance measures, and they have no generally

accepted academic measures to focus on as helpful tools in calcu-
lating employees' performance.[10] Why should administrators search
for such measures? Performance measures can mean only increased
responsibility; few people volunteer for that unless there are rewards to go with it. College faculty and administrators can act in
ways that employees at private companies might like to act but are
not allowed to because the market demands performance and even-
tually disciplines sloppy, unproductive practices.

Can Boards Perform Diligently?

College trustees are like the members of a corporate board of directors. They legally are the principals of the organization and thus
responsible for the successful completion of its mission. For a corporation, the mission is long-run profit maximization to benefit
shareholders. Fiascoes at Enron and other companies have made it
clear what happens when board members are inattentive or do not
understand what is happening within the organization they have an
obligation to oversee. Corrections are made.

When a company board does a poor job of hiring and monitoring top managers to enhance firm value, the stock price will be
lower than it would be if the company is in the hands of more competent managers. If the directors do not correct the situation, outsiders can mount an effort to gain control of the board, replace top
management, restructure the company, and enhance company performance. The history of takeovers indicates that most such decisions are justified; the firm or group that engineers the takeover im-
proves firm performance. If a mistake is made, those who
engineered the takeover suffer financial consequences.

Ownership, and the financial rewards and punishments it brings,
is key to the success of for-profit organizations and the wealth that
form of organization has generated for the world economy (Rajan
and Zingales 2003). Countries that lack private ownership of property are poor because resources are misallocated. They are not

allocated on the basis of the desires of customers looking to spend their hard-earned income, but are based on the decisions of political leaders and bureaucrats. Whether such leaders are elected or are there by dictatorship, top-down control of resources produces great inefficiencies compared to the results that emerge from for-profit organizations in competitive economies. Managers in such organizations have strong incentives to use resources wisely and respond to customers, or market discipline will be imposed.

For colleges, the mission is not to maximize profit, but rather, perhaps, to maximize the quality of their educational output over time. Colleges have no financial market that allows outsiders to evaluate performance or allows a takeover to be mounted to replace a poor-quality college board with one that demands better results from top management. There are no shareholders to sue board members who are negligent in performance of their duties. Poor management of resources at public colleges usually produces calls for more taxpayer money to solve the "underfunding" problem.

College trustees, although elected, are volunteers who must think it an honor to sit on the board, considering that it means a commitment of valuable time. Most trustees have no particular expertise in higher education and are passive, allowing administrators to run the show unless things seem to be getting grossly out of hand. Trustees rarely focus on the kind of objective measures available to guide corporate board members. They do study college finances because many board members understand accounting and can discern if the budget is balanced. Beyond financial statements, data on enrollment, and assorted rankings of uncertain value, board members must rely on impressions.

The Proper Role of Trustees

Just as a board has responsibility for the direction a corporation takes, the trustees of a private college are usually designated by its charter to be responsible for upholding the mission of the college and for ensuring its solvency. At state colleges, the power of trustees is determined by state law, but it can be extensive. As the trustee of one state university noted, trustees are usually legally "responsible for the academic *and* material well-being of their institutions" (de Russy 1996, 6, emphasis in original). Faculty and administrators tend to think of trustee guidance as meddling, but passivity by a board is an abdication of duty. Just as a corporate board cannot legally grant carte blanche power to the president, a college board should not grant too much authority to the president and should engage in substantive academic planning with the president and review performance on that basis.

Most trustees do not play an active role in supervising day-to-day academic matters, which would be inappropriate, but they should decide basic issues involving top personnel and the institution's mission. Some private colleges have a religious orientation; others have a fixed classical liberal arts program. Trustees define and enforce such missions, and they should ensure that administrators and faculty are on board with these missions or take their services elsewhere.[11] One reason presidents may not last long is because boards are not well informed or do not participate enough in the decision process, so they are mostly in a veto role when trouble is brewing. Trustee activism does not mean just being critical; it means being informed. But, unlike compensated boards of corporations, where members also face liability for failing in their duties, college board members are providing charity with almost no chance of liability for miserable decisions.

Presidents' Incentives

Presidents are generally in charge of putting out fires and keeping trouble to a minimum. Former president Gerhard Casper of Stanford University noted that "Many people think of universities as hierarchical because they have a president with a fancy title ... but they are not hierarchical. Power comes from the bottom up. The most important decisions are those concerning admissions, curriculum and faculty appointments, and these are areas where the university president has almost no power. In most circumstances, I'm the man with the pail and broom" (quoted in Honan 1994, 16).

Unlike private companies, where presidents are brought in and often given a specific charge—such as to shuck losing operations, streamline management, change service lines, and so forth—few college presidents are brought in and specifically charged with cutting losing academic departments or unloading unproductive faculty. Presidents who undertake efficiency or academically innovative moves without solid board support are likely to be headed for a shorter term in office than if they leave things pretty much as they are.

It is not uncommon for a college board to hire a president and charge that person with hard management missions; if the board members will back up the president during the grief that is sure to come, the president may get something done. But most boards allow themselves to be handed a list of presidential finalists by a faculty-dominated committee (at one university, the faculty committee gave the board a list with only one name, which the board simply rubberstamped [de Russy 1996, 6]). Faculty have little interest, especially in a committee setting, in offering candidates for president who are likely to be capable of rocking the faculty boat. The list is usually composed of administrators from other institutions who have succeeded—from the faculty perspective—by keeping the lid on problems rather than by dealing with hard issues that may require substantive change. Passive boards mean passive presidents. The status quo reigns.

To stay in a president's job generally means balancing the books, being a decent person who talks about commitment to excellence, and not pressing for substantive change. A passive board will find little reason to dump such a president. Presidents who press for change force trustees to make decisions on controversial matters about which they have little experience. Although trustees rarely think faculty members are right in their mewling, they have little incentive to bear the costs of an ongoing fight in which they will be branded publicly as Neanderthals for supposedly destroying academic quality and freedom. A common solution, because troublesome faculty rarely leave, is to dump the president and hope that the next one will avoid such disputes.

In sum, because of the choice process and governance method, college presidents can be expected to be less entrepreneurial or creative than presidents of private companies and to tolerate employees (faculty) who could be replaced by better employees for the same or lower salary. A company president has financial targets to work toward; a college president need only do no worse than similar colleges. At state colleges, presidents can point at the legislature for not granting their wish list in the proposed budget. With such minimal control, there is little ability to try to improve a college academically. Indeed, efforts to impose change usually means hell to pay with the faculty. A president's pay is not raised for generating or bearing grief. Much more than in the corporate sector, judgments by college trustees about presidents' performance is likely to based on "feelings" about how things are going.

College Administrators

The specialization of academic disciplines requires administrators to rely on the faculty to provide expert judgment about curriculum and other faculty. The same is true in private companies; the president relies on accountants to handle accounting and engineers to handle engineering. The key issues are: How much control will faculty have, how will control be exercised, and what incentives do they have?

The economic model of human behavior presumes that we all are driven by self-interest. In general, humans prefer more income (and other goodies) to less, less work to more, and more control to less. The greatest challenge of management is to harness these natural instincts—to give people incentives to use their creative abilities in a constructive manner that is in the best interest of the organization. Beneficial results do not emerge simply by wishing that all faculty will work hard for the common good.

Monitoring faculty is difficult. Simple measures such as number of students taught, number of hours spent in an office, or number of pages published may have little relationship to quality and effectiveness. Focusing on input measures, such as number of hours of this or that, can produce perverse results. The issue in education—as in most productive activity, but especially intellectual activity—is the quality of the results.

A great challenge in academic administrations is to hold *individuals* responsible for what they produce. Compared to workers on assembly lines, sales representatives, lawyers generating billable hours, and so forth, faculty enjoy a significant lack of personal accountability. Except in the case of publications, which involve particular standards, there are limited objective measures of productivity. To complicate oversight, responsibility can be masked by committee decisions, which is one reason colleges are dominated by committees. Some committees are useful, but our point is that faculty and administrators in colleges have strong incentives to make sure committees dominate most aspects of the organization.

Administrators can skirt responsibility by appointing committees, which reduces complaints by faculty about nondemocratic decision making, and then choosing among the options presented by the committee. Skillful administrators appoint committees they know are likely to produce the results desired; in any event, many hours of valuable time are consumed producing decisions that any one person with good sense could have generated more quickly. This process helps protect administrators from faculty criticism, but it does not always enhance the goals of the college.

The domination of decision making by college committees or even by informal consensus construction means that many hours of faculty and administrators' time are spent in nattering discussions—time they could have spent on matters related to teaching or research. This time is justified if the committees produce better decisions than individual decision makers can make on their own, but college committees tend to represent and perpetuate the status quo. Tomorrow looking like today is much more satisfying to most people than an uncertain future, especially one that may require them to work harder, such as in preparing new course material, with no expectation of higher compensation.

4

Eating the Fixed Pie

Imagine the following scenario. A division within General Motors comes up with a design for a new model. The managers of that division have evidence, based on surveys and the direction the automotive market has been moving, that the new model has a high probability of success. To produce it will require GM to shift resources within the organization. The resources would mostly likely be removed from a division that is not doing very well. It may not be doing well because it is not using resources effectively or it may simply be the victim of changing preferences by customers. No doubt there would be arguments within the company about the sensibility of such a move, but top management would probably reassign resources in the belief that the change would help generate a higher rate of return for the company than if resource allocation remained the same.

Within universities, especially public schools, this common-sense managerial model does not hold. Academic departments that have few customers are often propped up by departments that are attracting many student/customers. Shifting resources from poor-performing departments to high-performing departments is explosive within the university, and so highly risky for top management. The losers will fight hard to keep what they have, and enlist the support of other departments that fear that they could be seen as losers. The scramble for resources is greatly affected by internal politics that responds little to evidence of shifting market forces.

Most universities have a "democratic" model of faculty participation in governance. Committees at the faculty and administrative levels vote on just about everything. Hence, representatives from around the university get to vote on any proposal from any department—by, say, the criminology department to begin a master's program in crime scene investigation. The game is, of course, that other colleges want assurance that the university will not devote a larger share of its budget to a college that is proposing a new or expanded program. It does not matter if the proposed program is the greatest thing since sliced bread; faculty and administrators from other departments are likely to oppose a master's program in crime scene investigation if they think it might cost them any resources, no matter how beneficial the current use of university resources may be. Student or university welfare is not a concern. Faculty think of college budgets as a fixed pie to be sliced up, rather than as a pie to be made and expanded by contributions from all those who are supposed to help bake the pie.

This skewed decision process is worsened by policies in many states that require colleges to go to the state capital to lobby bureaucrats on state higher education commissions for new programs. Whether or not a proposed program may have merit matters little and, in most cases, is beyond the bureaucrats' ability to judge. The commission's main concerns are "duplication," cost, and political support for the proposal. To reduce the cost objection (the bureaucrats can usually measure only inputs or costs; they have little incentive or ability to try to measure outputs or benefits), colleges often claim that new programs will be "free." Administrators assert that they will shuffle around resources so that a new program will cost "nothing." If they tell the truth about program costs, they are less likely to be successful in getting bureaucratic approval.

To get an idea of how difficult it is to measure even seemingly simple things in universities (thereby compounding evaluation of managerial effectiveness), consider these examples. The AAUP claimed that for the years 1983 to 1993 the number of administrators at the University of Arizona increased 42 percent, but the university reported 3 percent fewer administrators; the truth appears to be in between (Beattie 1994, 11). Who is classified as what can be a matter of semantics. Full-time researchers may be listed as administrative personnel because they are not teaching faculty. When universities beg legislatures for money, they have incentives to miscount administrators. Similarly, how does one allocate overhead? In *Administrative Expenditures in Texas Public Universities*, the Texas Higher Education Coordinating Board asserts that "administrative expenditures per full-time equivalent student" in 1993 was only $337 per year at Texas Tech and $346 at East Texas State, but it was $1,997 at the University of Houston, Victoria. Similarly, Texas A&M claimed to have spent (in constant 1993 dollars) $1,871 per student in 1985, but only $652 per student in 1993 (Texas Higher Education Coordinating Board 1994, 12). It is not believable that administrative overhead was slashed by two-thirds at Texas A&M during those years or that Houston at Victoria really spent six times as much on overhead as did Texas Tech. Such numbers are meaningless for comparison purposes, yet administrators have strong incentives to devote substantial time crafting such reports to help sway legislators in the direction administrators want allocations to go.

The duplication concern has some merit given the current method of state appropriations, but it would have little merit if public colleges, like private colleges, had to compete rather than be granted protection by the state higher education cartel manager, the Commission on Higher Education. No doubt restaurants, physicians, or any other service provider would like a state agency to decide when there were "enough" providers of something. Burger King would always argue against allowing Wendy's to open a franchise nearby, and physicians would argue against allowing more doctors to open their offices in towns where there were "enough" doctors. Similarly, a state college that has an engineering school prefers to be the only one in the state because then it has a lock on students and faces less competition.

Because the state helps foot the bill for state colleges, and because the primary measure that legislators use is dollar inputs, there is good reason to be wary of new programs proposed by state colleges. On the other hand, from university administrators' perspective, any program the state will pay for is worth asking for, even if the program makes little sense academically. So if the "experts" in the capital want more engineering programs to "boost" economic development, proposals will come flooding in from colleges whether they make sense or not.

Share and Share Alike

A favorite topic in academics is "shared governance," which means "democratic" control of a university by faculty (Gerber 2001). As former Harvard dean Henry Rosovsky notes, "more democracy is not necessarily better" (1990, 265). Contrary to what many faculty think, they are not hired to determine general university policy. "Faculty members are invited to teach and do research and to set educational policy in their sphere of knowledge" (Rosovsky 1990, 266). The notion that the faculty possess some sort of collective wisdom that makes decision making about university operation democratic is nonsense. Many faculty can offer useful input on issues, but in most instances such opinions should be advisory. There is a conflict of interest between faculty's personal interests and the college's long-term interests.

Democratically controlled colleges and departments within colleges will tend to represent the "average" faculty preference. This fact is seen most easily in pay-raise matters. Left to a faculty vote, across-the-board equal pay increases, not merit raises, are likely to dominate. Administrators would rather have more substantial leeway in raises so that the less-productive faculty can be given nothing (to encourage their departure or to convince them to work harder) and the more productive can be given rewards.

Approximately 40 percent of faculty nationwide are unionized, primarily at state colleges.[12] If this figure rises, college education will become even more stultified and bureaucratized, and public colleges will be little more than years thirteen through sixteen in a state-run K–16 education system. Unionized colleges mean that administrators (and boards) have even less control over the structure of a college and its faculty.[13] Even if a faculty is not unionized, empirical studies confirm the notion that the more power the faculty are given in administrative decision making in a college, the lower the quality of the college (McCormick and Meiners 1988).

When average faculty preferences dominate college decisions, resources are likely to be allocated on an "equitable" basis, such as everyone gets their way paid to two professional meetings a year. Professor A, a recognized expert in a field, may be invited to go to numerous major meetings as a speaker, but Professor B, who produces nothing, volunteers to give a couple minutes' worth of comments at low-level meetings. With the same resources to support four trips, a sensible administrator would prefer to give A three or four trips and B one or none. The college's reputation is enhanced more by having Professor A appear at more meetings; Professor A is also less likely to get bid away to another college that offers more support for such events and rewards good work. But administrators who discriminate on the basis of productivity may face the wrath of less-productive faculty, so equality for all is likely to be the rule.

Similarly, shared resources are usually distributed on an equality basis, such as secretarial assistance; everyone has the same right of time usage, so the most productive faculty do not get enough help, whereas the unproductive faculty waste secretarial time having trivial matters processed. An irony of computers is that the most productive faculty have tended to move to producing all of their own work on a computer; unproductive faculty have not figured out how to use them and are more likely to rely on costly secretarial help for their meager output. Requests to the library for new books are treated the same whether they are from a productive professor, who actually reads and uses material, or from a slacker who has not read a scholarly book in years but goes through the motions of being intellectually alert.

A classic example of faculty democracy run amok, which produces results that are inconsistent with the fostering of cutting-edge knowledge, is in how many colleges distribute summer research grants. Unlike the National Science Foundation, which uses peer reviews by authorities in the fields in which grants are being requested, many universities have a university-wide faculty committee distribute grant money to faculty who apply. The bizarre spectacle then ensues in which economists and historians sit in judgment on the relative merits of proposals from faculty in pediatric nursing, chemistry, and sociology. Almost no one on the committee is competent to judge the merit of the proposals, yet the members solemnly make pronouncements on subjects about which they know almost nothing.

When employees (faculty) determine university policy by democratic voting, the most unproductive member of the faculty has the same weight as a Nobel Prize winner. Hence, faculty of average and below average quality, which by definition means at least half the faculty, lobby hard for more and more issues to be decided by democratic votes and for decisions to be taken to committees, not administrators.

Playing Politics

The committee decision-making problem is compounded by the fact that the faculty who are willing to accept committee assignments, or who lobby for election to large committees that consume significant time, such as the faculty senate, are often below-average-quality faculty. The best faculty are busy teaching, writing, or participating in external activities. Competent faculty, who of course have the best job opportunities, have little desire to spend afternoons trapped in conference rooms with blowhards who take hours to make pompous pronouncements about any issue. Faculty committees are invariably overrepresented by those who have incentives to lobby to keep the faculty in control of as many resources and decisions as possible and to oppose change in general. Their claim to fame is "service" to the college, not teaching or research. Administrators know that these faculty members will spend countless hours arguing about resource allocation so they get their share of the pie—and, hence, the misguided focus on tenure much of the time.

Many faculty resist change at a college because change, by definition, means more work and greater uncertainty about the future. Especially at public colleges, where the state can be relied on to send support year after year to maintain the status quo, the safest bet is for faculty to support administrators who leave things alone and, even better, spend their time raising extra money to support what is going on. As Robert Zemsky, the head of the Institute for Research on Higher Education at the University of Pennsylvania, once noted, "senior professors lack any financial incentive to support [change]." That is, if nothing extra is being offered to them, faculty see no reason to cooperate with anyone who threatens life as it is; their attitude is "why cooperate ... I'm outta here in 10 or 11 years ... so why should I bother?" (quoted in Honan 1994, 18).

Faculty, like most employees, instinctively resist change. Administrators' lives are easier if they give in to faculty desire for tomorrow to look like today. As Don Paarlberg, a leading agricultural economist, has noted, many parts of agricultural colleges make no sense given the modern structure of agriculture, yet the government keeps pumping money into academic departments with very few students (1992, 45). Supported by such political largess, agriculture colleges often have programs in agricultural business that should be a part of regular business education, just as agricultural biology departments should be merged into regular biology departments. We know of schools that have agriculture departments with more tenured professors than undergraduate majors. But what would make for a better use of resources in terms of student demand is largely irrelevant when colleges can get funds for programs regardless of whether or not students are enrolled.

Risk Avoidance

Dismissing the worst—that is, most unproductive—tenured faculty members, which is a small percentage of the total, sends chills through the ranks of everyone who worries that they also are seen as, or might become, deadwood. If faculty want the assurance that tenure in practice means a life sinecure, which is *not* what tenure grants legally, they have strong incentives, often under the guise of academic freedom and within faculty committees that wield too much power, to protest any move against incompetent faculty. Many people in a college, including the students and secretaries, know who the worst faculty members are, but the worst provide the safety net for those who are a little bit better, so faculty in general have little incentive to lobby to get rid of their worst peers. Unlike in a for-profit organization, where bad employees can cost everyone money, at a college an unproductive professor does not directly lower the income of other faculty. It is comforting to know that if you want to become a slacker, you are very unlikely to be subject to dismissal. Hence, even productive faculty may not support moves to replace incompetent faculty.

Colleges, more so than businesses, often hire outsiders as presidents. Most presidents resign under some duress, so the trustees, looking to "solve" the management problem, bring in an outsider. There is some merit to this approach because the outsider might bring some fresh thinking and has no ties to the incumbent power structure within the college. The down side is that the new person must spend time learning about personality conflicts and problems before he or she can address the more significant management issue; by the time he or she is up to speed, the honeymoon is over.

Some new presidents, knowing the precarious nature of a position that relies more on personal loyalty than on measured results, try to protect themselves by appointing new administrators. That is why some new presidents replace all vice presidents or deans. They hire a new crew, all of whom owe their jobs to the president. It is a good self-protection strategy, but not usually sensible because good administrators can be lost. Candidates for president from within a university face the problem that they are already well known, and if they have instituted change, they have probably made some faculty angry. Every real and alleged mistake is well known and discussed. Outside candidates are not well known to people at a college, so they have fewer warts exposed. In addition, search firms that are paid to generate candidates for college president job openings are more likely to champion outsiders.

Let It Be

Life without change seems less risky and easier. Many faculty prefer that tomorrow (or the next decade) look like yesterday. Vanderbilt University economists did a study of change at colleges and found that "it took, on average almost 26 years for half of the institutions in our survey to adopt the 30 innovations that we studied. ... It took an average of 40 years for half the institutions ... to adopt the five financial innovations that we studied." Why are they so slow? "It appears that colleges and universities are indeed insulated from many competitive pressures; they have no stockholders and their governing boards have few ready measures to judge performance. Declining enrollments signal difficulties but tell presidents and boards little about how to improve their institutions. Trustees, who work with vague and sometimes conflicting goals, seldom provide incentives for administrators to pursue innovation aggressively"(Siegfried, Getz, and Anderson 1995, 56).

That is, not only can curriculum be stagnant or unresponsive to student needs, but colleges themselves are incredibly slow to adopt efficiency tools, such as computerized financial controls, that no one would claim has anything to do with academic freedom. Many colleges still shuffle around pieces of carbon paper and triplicate forms like the army did in World War II. When administrators suggest change, they are given a laundry list of reasons why it cannot work or is not allowed (which is sometimes actually true because many states have archaic procedures preventing internal agency reform), or they are simply stonewalled by stubborn employees. As the Vanderbilt economists note, because administrators do not own stock in colleges, they do not have strong reasons to anger employees by insisting on implementing new and more efficient methods of operation.

Consider the grief encountered in these examples of attempted change at various universities. In 1993, the administration of the University of Pennsylvania abolished three departments (religious studies, American civilization, and regional science), presumably owing to low demand and perhaps to academic weakness by university standards. Even though no faculty were fired because they were offered assignments in other departments, many unaffected faculty presented strong opposition to this change (Chait 1995, 1). Just the *mention* of rearrangements, to say nothing of dismissals, sets off faculty furor. Too often administrators back down rather than take the heat. For example, when in the face of severe budget problems the chancellor of the City University of New York, a multicampus system, proposed to eliminate approximately two hundred degree programs that were unneeded or had low enrollments, six college faculties voted "no confidence" in her, and she was forced to backpedal (Honan 1994, 16).

When the chancellor of the University of Maine tried to introduce interactive televised education around the state, primarily so that residents of rural towns would have access to Maine courses, he was forced to resign because the board of trustees allowed the faculty union to control the agenda.[14] Faculty were concerned that distance education could reduce the demand for their services, so there was strong opposition to increased service to citizens of the state.

Maine faculty also opposed the chancellor's proposal to give Maine college students exit exams to try to determine how much students had learned. Heaven forbid! The new chancellor— brought in by the trustees, who capitulated to pacify the faculty— promised that distance learning would have a limited role. The head of the faculty union threatened that if it did not, the new chancellor would "have trouble with the faculty" (*Portland Press Herald* 1995, 1).

Practical Differences Between Private and Public Colleges

Would state colleges be more effective if they were run like private colleges? There is evidence that despite the inefficiencies suffered by non-profit organizations compared to for-profit organizations, non-profit colleges have some advantages over public colleges. Let us consider some of the differences between the two sets of institutions.

Both public and private colleges have boards of trustees. Whereas private college boards are legally the principals of the organizations and may control the college as they think best for it to fulfill its educational mission, public colleges are state agencies. The boards of public colleges usually have power to appoint the president, but they are representatives of the state to oversee the agency on behalf of the citizens. How much authority the trustees have is a matter of state law: in some states, they have substantial power, almost like private college trustees; in other states, the boards are largely ceremonial, and real power resides at a central state agency, such as a board or commission of higher education.

State colleges must follow state laws governing spending and employment. Just as the Pentagon is famous for overpriced equipment and the U.S. Park Service for million dollar outhouses, universities often pay more for buildings and supplies than if they were not subject to intricate state rules and political meddling. Colleges (and other state agencies) may spend more in personnel overhead preparing requests for bids and processing the bids than the stuff being bought is worth. Invoices for trivial purchases may have to clear six levels of approval. Such rules are usually imposed in the wake of someone doing something wrong, but efforts to avoid occasional theft or bonehead decisions often result in high bureaucratic costs for all purchases in order to prevent minor losses. Elaborate bidding procedures make many companies avoid dealing with state institutions because the rules are so complex. It makes purchasing less, not more competitive. Even if rules are created with the best intentions, they impose costs in price paid and overhead staff needed to ensure compliance. College administrators have little control over such costs.

Private colleges face fewer legal constraints on buying practices and other features of operation. They set their tuition rates and offer scholarships to students as they see fit, given market conditions. State colleges charge a tuition set by legislative rules. Scholarships, unless funded by a special pot of appropriations, which many states have, must be funded by private donations. Hence, state colleges find it more difficult than private schools to change the way they operate and the way they respond to market conditions.

The fact that public colleges have a difficult time attracting academic stars illustrates their lack of flexibility. Nobel Prize winners tend to be concentrated at private colleges that can pay what their services command. State colleges, if for nothing more than political reasons, usually cannot go over some salary level and usually have less flexibility in the terms of employment than private colleges. It is no surprise that the top-ranked colleges in the nation, both at the graduate research level and at the undergraduate teaching level, are private colleges. Their trustees can allow administrators to be more creative than is generally the case at public colleges, even though public colleges have the benefit of state appropriations.

Although commanding less than a quarter of the student market, in general, private colleges offer a broader range of alternatives than do public colleges, discriminate more on tuition, and are more creative in faculty contracts. Trustees of private colleges can exert more control over what goes on at their colleges than is usually the case at public colleges, but both sets of colleges suffer from the same general internal problems with respect to faculty incentives, although private colleges suffer these problems more from trustee indifference or ignorance rather than for external political reasons.

5

Managing Faculty
as a Valued Resource

Faculty evaluation is touchy business. As at any place of employment, no one enjoys being compared to other employees, unless one is always ranked at the top. If productivity can be measured by sales, number of calls made, number of widgets produced, and so forth, there is little room for disagreement—the highest producers get the largest rewards. In the academic market, competition among colleges and nonacademic employers helps set the wage rate. Hence, new Ph.D.s in engineering or chemistry, who have good nonacademic opportunities, must be paid more than Ph.D.s in history and other such fields, where many compete for few opportunities. But how do you decide annual rewards among a group of professors once they are hired?

Teaching quality is difficult but not impossible to measure. Student evaluations are useful and could be used more effectively, but student evaluations are not the end all. Students know a lazy teacher when they see one, but they often cannot discriminate between a knowledgeable instructor and one with little substance but more personality. All faculty have had a student tell them how wonderful Professor So-and-So is, when they know that So-and-So is among the least intellectually competent of the faculty. As with minimally competent physicians whose good bedside manner can fool many patients, glib instructors can fool students. At the other extreme, an incompetent teacher can be a tough grader and claim that his toughness is the reason students do not like him.

Knowledge of teaching competence is best determined by those with expertise in the same field. Professors of accounting generally know who among them know their stuff. Simple measures, such as numbers of students taught or quality of student evaluations, do not tell the whole story. Just as we rely on good law firms to provide us with competent counsel to handle a particular case, we should generally rely on faculty and administrator judgments about who is competent in the classroom.

If we want to encourage competent teaching, administrators must have the final say, even if this means overriding student evaluations of popular professors. Such instances provoke "scandals" from time to time when a college denies tenure to a popular teacher; the students may think the teacher swell, but administrators and colleagues may have found the teacher to be of dubious intellectual ability (or moral fiber). Style is nice, but substance is more important in higher education.

The problem with teaching, then, is to give faculty an incentive to do a good job consistently, to improve lectures, to give students assignments and exams that may be time-consuming to grade (and that most students resent) but are better teaching tools, and so forth. Private colleges, in general, demand better teaching than do public colleges, but the basic problem is inherent to both sets of institutions. Unless faculty income is tied to substantive teaching performance, there is little incentive to invest time and effort in effective teaching. Even if good teaching makes students happy, how can faculty capture gains other than the value of popularity?

Do Teaching and Research Conflict?

Good teaching is hard to capitalize into pay. From a faculty member's perspective, therefore, even time spent on committees that try to grab college resources may be time well spent. As noted earlier, committee work and on-campus politics are most likely to appeal to faculty who have, on average, less than average abilities. Contrary to common perception, scholarly output by faculty is a good thing; it is demonstrated evidence of knowledge and, perhaps as important, evidence that the faculty member is continuing to think and work in his field, rather than just repeating old knowledge. The issue is the *balance* between teaching and publication. Colleges do not want professors to maximize publication output by shirking on teaching quality. High-quality colleges that have faculty with excellent publication records also demand quality teaching. Good teaching and research should go together.

At leading universities, the research stars are often among the best teachers, at least in advanced courses. Productive researchers may not be the best at putting on a show, but because they usually teach graduate courses and upper-division undergraduates, showmanship is not as important as substantive knowledge that actually is at the cutting edge of a discipline. Good researchers are often effective teachers because they are on top of developments in their field and are constantly excited by knowledge.

However, unless teaching is rewarded, the incentive for faculty can be to maximize research output. Unlike good teaching, which rarely gets one a marketable reputation, a good publication record keeps one more mobile in the job market. If a professor's current employer does not provide adequate rewards, a good publication record is evidence of scholarly knowledge that can be demonstrated to other colleges interested in hiring new faculty.

From the perspective of trustees and administrators, who want productive faculty, the problem is to get faculty interested in teaching better and politicking less or, in a few cases, in teaching better and doing a little less research. From the perspective of the institution, the most destructive faculty is the one who does not teach well, does little or no research, but spends significant time on committees and campus politics. These faculty are administrators' nightmares. The rotten wood know that unless they commit a crime, they are unlikely to be fired, so they invest their time, at college expense, lobbying for more control of resources.

Problem Child as Hero

Unproductive faculty have weak academic records, so they are unlikely to be offered another academic job. They are most likely to spend their time fighting for resources and resisting change. Administrators who cross them better be ready to do battle with those who have nothing but time on their hands to spend stirring up trouble. When a nasty scrap occurs between administrators and some faculty, the public often just sees a professor who claims to be crusading for academic freedom or quality teaching. The media and outsiders do not know one physics professor from another and therefore do not know if faculty rotten wood are leading the charge against proposed changes. It always makes good news copy to have an outspoken professor attacking "waste" by an administration that "does not care" about students. Such public blathering also provides the professor with the possible cover of claiming retaliation from administration in violation of First Amendment rights in case of serious trouble to his or her position.

As anyone experienced in media relations knows, the media rarely gets news right and should not be expected to. Reporters have limited time for any story, are looking for sensationalism, and have no insights about the matter at hand. Rosovsky notes that one day he heard on the radio that he had been reprimanded for sexually harassing a student. In fact, the day before, he had reprimanded a faculty member for the activity reported. "That the story was seriously garbled by the media I had learned to expect" (1990, 38). Trying to correct bad reporting produces either no results or even more hostility because the reporter's intelligence or integrity is questioned, so it is best for administrators to ignore most such matters, which enforces the public notion that administrators are a pretty dubious bunch and that some outspoken "crusading" professor is to be admired.

Administrators who want an easier life do not take on the worst-performing employees; they make peace instead. Faculty generally think well of do-nothing administrators or of administrators who devote all their time to fund-raising rather than to enhancing the use of resources at hand, which may mean getting more work out of the current employees and driving out the worst employees. Hence, trustees have a hard time discerning if administrators liked by faculty are liked because they are so skillful that productivity improvements can be made without upsetting people who do not care to work more for the same pay, or because they are not doing much. As one of our colleagues once noted, well-regarded university presidents often look distinguished, speak with apparent authority, but do little of substance.

Make Change Pay

In the private sector, change is a fact of life. Call it total quality management, continuous improvement, or reengineering, companies either change and improve or go out of business. The market is tough; if IBM had not cut back its work force, dumped nonproductive divisions, and made other hard changes, one of the most successful firms in the world in the 1960s and 1970s would have died in the 1990s. Its board and managers did not enjoy the hardship some employees endured and the difficult changes to which those remaining had to adapt, but these changes brought the company back to life. If IBM had been run like a university, the company would now be a distant memory. A better analogy to universities may be the former steel giants that were strangled by union work rules; the union workers were like professors who resist increases in productivity and will not accept the fact that the glory days, when Ph.D.s were in hot demand in many disciplines, are over. Real wages in most academic disciplines have fallen; people of at least equal competence would do the same job for less. Colleges that can adapt will be more successful than those unable to change the incentives facing the biggest cost item—faculty.

Colleges have seen productivity improvements in many areas. Food service has improved as private firms have taken over from college-run kitchens; college-run dorms have been replaced by privately operated living quarters; computers have allowed registration lines to be eliminated; libraries are hooking into computer databases. Academic departments, however, are still run much like they were in 1955. There was nothing efficient about them then, and there is even less efficient about them today as the education market becomes more competitive.

There is no doubt that *most* faculty provide good value—they do a solid job teaching and plug away at research. They are not the problem. But a portion of the faculty at any college could be replaced with higher-quality people at the same or lower price. Tenure does not prevent such people from being replaced; the problem is the nonprofit nature of higher education. Given that there is little likelihood of a significant move to for-profit higher education, the challenge for trustees and administrators is to concentrate on ways to give all faculty incentives to perform better. Moving to enhance faculty productivity has *nothing* to do with academic freedom. Academic freedom was never intended to be a license for sorry work habits; it concerns the freedom to teach in the classroom in one's area of expertise, within the general standards set for students at a college. Educational productivity can be improved and academic freedom increased at the same time. Easier said than done. If we knew *how* to resolve this extraordinarily difficult management issue, we would be wealthy consultants. Our mission here is to note that the common focus on tenure is misdirected. Next we move to a discussion of some possible reforms that have been tried or might be tried and review the possible merits among them.

6

Reforming Tenure
or University Structure?

Because tenure is perceived as a major cause of slothful
and bad behavior in universities, it is sometimes the focus of attack.
As we have discussed, tenure as it exists is not a barrier to dismissing or disciplining poorly performing or badly behaving faculty
members. Because of that, we think the well-intended efforts to
"reform" tenure draw attention away from larger issues that should
be addressed in the structure of universities. Consider what happened when the regents of the University of Minnesota considered
rewriting the tenure rules (see the *Minneapolis Star-Tribune* 1996,
various issues, for the material given in this discussion).

In late 1995, the regents of the University of Minnesota de-
clared their interest in reforming tenure. The faculty senate
then "reworked" tenure, the result being—surprise, surprise—
"no significant loosening of the tenure code." In June 1996,
the president told the regents that the entire top administration opposed laying off professors who taught in programs that
were being abolished.

Making no progress with the faculty or administration, the regents, who had worked with academic consultants, made key features of their proposal public: (1) tenured faculty could be fired if
their programs were abolished; (2) tenured faculty with poor performance could suffer pay cuts; and (3) faculty who did not "maintain ... a proper attitude of industry and cooperation with others
within and without the University community" could be disciplined; faculty could also be fired for "grave misconduct."

The faculty response was predictable. The Faculty Consultative Committee said that the regents proposal "undermines ... academic freedom" and destroys the "ability to serve the citizens of Minnesota." Without blushing, the committee also asserted that "Academic freedom is of primary benefit not to professors, but to society."

What resulted? In September 1996, the president opposed the regents' proposed changes, saying "compromise by the faculty will hurt the university." The media reported, "administration officials remain staunchly behind the faculty, even though they work for the regents." In October, Governor Arne Carlson, who claimed he favored tenure reform, said that the fight was hurting the university (whatever that means). Regent Jean Keffeler, seen as a primary force behind the tenure change proposal, resigned.[15] In November, the regents threw in the towel, although they never voted on the issue. When it was announced that the regents decided it no longer needed the services of its expert consultant on tenure, Professor Richard Chait of Harvard, the faculty "cheered" (Magner 1997, A10).

The dean of the Law School, attempting to mediate the matter, proposed a modification to the three-point plan. No layoffs would occur when a program was abolished unless a professor refused to be reassigned; faculty members must agree to pay cuts; pay can be cut for a poorly performing faculty member, but only if his or her peers agree with the cut; and the notion of a "cooperative attitude" would be dropped. Many faculty denounced even this tepid plan. A moratorium on action was called in the university as the faculty considered unionization, except in the Law School. The Law School adopted a tenure policy in 1997 allowing tenure to be revoked in cases of "grave misconduct manifestly inconsistent with continued faculty appointment," with such determination to be made by peer (faculty) review. This trivial change in policy, consistent with AAUP tenure guidelines, was viewed as a major event ("Tenure Is No Longer Untouchable" 1997, 10).

The point of this story is to look at the grief incurred by unpaid trustees. Even administrators who attempted to discuss a watered-down change in tenure policy were vilified. You can be sure that if they ever apply for an administrative job at another university, enough of the faculty there would fight the appointment that it simply would not happen. Tinkering with the status quo is personally costly to trustees and can wreck administrative careers. Again, we suggest that tenure rules as they exist are adequate to do the job—if enforced. Other structural changes should be considered to enhance competition within and across universities.

Admit It: We're Bureaucrats

Most students attend colleges run by state employees. Colleges are no less bureaucracies than are highway departments and local public schools. Private universities do not suffer all the problems built into an agency that relies on legislators for a budget, but the lack of a profit measure makes it difficult for any nonprofit organization to know how well it is doing. Balancing the budget of a college does not mean a good job is being done. Monitoring nonprofit organizations so that the people running them have incentives to do a good job and make constant improvements is a truly difficult management task that has never yet been mastered.

As Peter Drucker notes, most government agencies operate the same today as when they were created decades ago. Businesses must continuously improve—lower costs, improve service—or lose to competition. Government agencies *talk* about doing that, but mostly they do no more than just talk. To know if you are improving, you have to have benchmarks to measure quality enhancements or cost efficiencies. "Continuous improvement and benchmarking ... require radical changes in policies and practices which the bureaucracy, the employees' unions, and Congress would all fiercely resist" (1995, 52).

Most voters do not want to get rid of many government services; they want more *effective* government for the money. But changing established programs meets with strong resistance. When change is mentioned, opponents can be expected to claim that all benefits will be destroyed. Opposition comes from those who earn their living in the current system and from members of the legislature who benefit from the current system because they are in charge of controlling the flow of benefits, including new building contracts and other goodies for their districts (see Meiners and Miller 1996). Thus, understanding that change in the method of service delivery may be beneficial can be much easier than actually dealing with the political reality of implementing change.

Education Is Not "Different"

Those of us who are state college faculty and administrators do not like to admit that the theory of bureaucracy applies every bit as much to us as it does to the Postal Service, the IRS, and the drivers' license bureau. Employees of private colleges work for nonprofit charities, which have many characteristics of bureaucracies, so some of the discussion here applies to them, but our immediate focus is on state colleges. The assertion that "education is different," and therefore that faculty and administrators of colleges are not really like bureaucrats, is either a disingenuous effort to try to fool the voters or self-delusion (cognitive dissonance, as psychologists might say) about our real place as employees of government agencies.

Little scholarly work has been done about the problems of universities as bureaucracies. Given the mass of academic publications, this is a bit odd, but it is difficult to be objective about things in which we are intimately involved. It is easier to think about how the highway department works or the incentives in the Pentagon than it is to think about our own bailiwick. Some books about higher education are histories or descriptions of things as they are.

Other books are stories about "crisis in the ivory tower" owing to an alleged lack of resources from ignorant legislators and an uncaring public. Others concern the low education standards imposed by crazed faculty who like to show pornographic movies to students for college credit.

Our focus is on the problems that emerge from the incentive structure of a college bureaucracy. The economic theory of bureaucracy explains that bureaucrats have incentives to generate the largest possible budget (see Niskanen 1971). This theory is no surprise to voters or legislators who understand the political process. It helps to explain why state universities are large relative to private universities. The political reward is larger for larger volume; that is, giant universities have larger political constituents who carry more clout in the legislature.

Administrators in larger state universities are paid higher salaries than those in smaller colleges. Harvard and Yale are big by private university standards, but they are small compared to successful public schools such as Berkeley, Michigan, and Illinois. Economic theory suggests that state universities are larger than they would be if they were not bureaucracies. This conclusion is evidenced by the fact the highest-quality private universities could certainly expand their enrollments to forty thousand, but have rejected that opportunity.

One empirical study found that public colleges "employ roughly 40% more labor than the private colleges for the same size capital stock" (Orzechowski 1977, 257). The prices paid for labor were roughly the same at both the public and private colleges (the labor market is competitive), but the public colleges had larger staffs for the same size facilities. This finding is consistent with other studies of private versus public producers of various services, although in most studies the other producers are for-profit organizations. Nevertheless, whether it is airlines, garbage collection, or fire protection, the private providers produce more output per employee than do public bureaucracies in the same line of work.[16]

Theory and the Real World

Academics are often irritated by critics who say something like, "Well, that may be fine in theory, but the real world is different." That is often an ignorant attack on scientific method. Not all theories are correct, but they are indispensable in helping us to model and understand our incredibly complex world. Theorizing is how science advances. Of relevance here is what management and economic theory has to contribute to our understanding of organizations so that we can apply it to universities to help them perform better.

As Alfred Chandler noted years ago about multidivisional corporations (which can be thought to include universities), managers delegate most decision-making responsibilities to divisional managers, minimizing their direct involvement in strategy (see Chandler 1962). Universities do this; presidents delegate most decision making to "divisional managers" such as deans and department heads. A decision to allocate resources to a new product usually requires approval of corporate staff. Similarly, in universities, upper administration must sign-off on new "products." The corporate staff acts as an entrepreneur and creates value by allocating and monitoring capital and specific managerial skills to pursue certain strategies (see Chandler 1991). Again, universities are somewhat like this in that faculty and administrators propose changes or new ventures that upper administration must approve when resources are to be committed.

When corporate executives cannot effectively monitor divisional behavior by accounting or financial measures, they are more likely to be involved in business-level decisions (see Hill, Hitt, and Hoskisson 1992). Here is where colleges begin to diverge from the organizational model. Accounting and financial measures are of little use in universities other than for current budget-control purposes. They tell us almost nothing about program quality, so administrators must use subjective evaluations to decide where the

resources will be allocated. Yet, at state universities, top administrators rarely allocate resources based on evaluations of different divisions' performance or based on estimates about future demand.
Similarly, trustees are even less involved in planning the future direction of the institution than are directors of private firms in making decisions about these firms' future.

Divisions in a private firm often try to get more resources allocated to them than makes sense for the firm as a whole. Executives
must resolve these interdivisional competitions for resources. The
more difficulty management has in measuring capabilities, the
greater the difficulty market governance has in allocating resources
efficiently (see Alchian and Demsetz 1972, a pioneering work in
economic theory). Corporate staff must exercise more personal
control to monitor division behavior when assessments are difficult
to make. Academic units' performance and output are very difficult
to measure; such assessment is largely a judgment call. But unlike
executives in private for-profit organizations who rely more on
their judgment when there are no good hard measures to go on,
college administrators rarely exercise much leadership about major
production decisions.

College administrators are aware of their problems and, no
doubt, are reminded of it by some boards. Administrators take
good-faith stabs at adopting managerial tools. One story on point
is relayed in the book *On Q: Causing Quality in Higher Education,* which discusses examples of colleges that asserted they would
adopt total quality management or other management techniques (Seymour 1993, 35ff.). Meaningful adoption of managerial
methods happens with varying degrees of success in corporations.
In the case of colleges, the author found that the discussion is
all talk about commitment to managerial improvement, with no
concrete results.

Like most administrators, we have suffered through pointless
management seminars. Regardless of how substantive or well-
intended such seminars are, there must be an incentive to follow

through in practice. Having administrators sit around and assert their commitment to excellence is pap. Because college administrators keep their jobs largely at the courtesy of their employees (the faculty), there may be a revolt that costs them their jobs if they try to impose managerial discipline or change. Some administrators exhort the troops to fall in line, be good citizens, get with the program that will benefit them, and so forth, but most faculty sit on their hands knowing that this too shall pass. Experienced employees in bureaucracies know that if they just hunker down, the administrators with fancy ideas about change will soon be gone.

Of course, some programs clearly have good results, which faculty eagerly point to as evidence of excellence. For example, an accounting department can look at the pass rates of their students on the CPA exam and at the percentage of students hired by the big public accounting firms. These methods are not the only measures of success for an accounting department, but they are a good place to start. Other disciplines and colleges as a whole could have their feet held to the fire if there were more hard measures of output.

Tom Peters says that what he stresses for organizations are dynamics (constant renewal) and innovation. *In Search of Excellence* stresses "autonomy and entrepreneurship" within the organization—changing to do better than competitors and to satisfy customers (1996, 239). Universities tend to be the opposite of dynamic and entrepreneurial, yet they are a primary source of training in our information-based economy. The contrast between a company such as IBM, which had to remake itself in response to changes in information processing, and universities, which have the same structure and often the same curriculum as they did thirty years ago, could not be more confounding. Institutions filled with bright, innovative people are ironically the most conservative and resistant to change.

Harvard Business School professor Rosabeth Kanter notes that as information becomes more important, organizations need more concepts, competence, and connections:

> These assets rely on human capabilities: creativity and imagination, teaching and learning, trust and respect.... Large organizations must tear down the confining vertical structures that shape bureauspace—skyscrapers, towers, silos, walls, and tunnel vision. They must behave like networks of smaller companies, liberating people to think like entrepreneurs but connecting them to share knowledge and to form a fluid array of project teams, within the company and with partners. (1996, 248)

This restructuring is not easy to accomplish in private firms and is far more difficult in bureaucracies. It will not happen simply by telling faculty and administrators about the need to get with modern managerial techniques. Incentives must be changed. That is, university managers and faculty must have *reasons* to want to do what the buyers of higher education pay them to do. They should want to give value for the dollar, knowing that if they do not, support will be lost to the many other colleges out there. Improvements occur in business organizations; they can occur in universities, too.

7

Internal Reforms

Trustees must play a lead role in working with administrators to allow reforms to be instituted, unthwarted by faculty tantrums about change. Trustees do not want to run the internal university details, but they should set the stage to empower faculty to work for changes in their areas of expertise without endless bureaucratic interference. When public colleges boom and money pours in, new programs are added. Faculty are creative at inventing new programs to tap into such money. When budgets are tight, one or two programs may go, but, unlike most shrinking businesses, colleges generally change very little. They tend to cut budgets across the board because administrators suffer less grief in doing so than if they fire incompetent professors and abolish programs not in demand. Faculty have little incentive to cooperate with change. Change means work, and, even worse, it threatens the status quo and job security.

Most colleges have rigid degree requirements, especially in terms of required classes in individual departments, based on program models that evolved during the boom days of higher education decades ago. Tampering with the status quo is risky to faculty, so they generally oppose change. Outmoded courses and degree programs live on. Bad teaching is not punished. College administrators rarely impose change or discipline the slackers, unless a higher authority forces them to do so, because the administration process does not encourage entrepreneurial behavior and provides little incentive for administrators to act like we presume managers should act. As discussed earlier, it is not in their interest to be known as tough-minded decision makers who threaten the status quo. Let's consider how to change some incentives to address various problems.

Stale Curriculum

Most colleges historically were liberal-arts schools with strong religious affiliations. They had missions that were fairly well understood. This is very different from large state universities, with hundreds of professors in diverse disciplines who have no substantive knowledge of each other's fields. At a large state school, money from the legislature arrives in lump sums based on assorted formulas and political influence. No one professor has any impact on the future of the college, so there is little reason to worry about his or her performance, except when pay raises are based on comparisons among the faculty (which they rarely are). Despite their lack of expertise outside of their own fields, professors control their peers by voting on program and course proposals. It is as if a corporate marketing department had to get approval by the accountants before being allowed to change the content of advertising campaigns. Contrary to general opinion, by reducing "democratic" voting controls over curriculum, faculty would actually have more freedom to experiment with course offerings and degree programs that appeal to students.

At most universities, faculty committees determine the fate of curriculum changes proposed by their peers. Even to change a catalog description of an existing course may require both a memo justifying the change and approval by the faculty member's departmental curriculum committee. That is probably sensible, but the proposal then goes to a college curriculum committee, where each department has a vote. Next it goes to a university curriculum committee, which is composed of representatives of various colleges. A course modification that may be fully understood by the professor suggesting the change and by his or her department must thus be approved by people ignorant about the matter and who could not really care less about what is taught in that course— unless it might somehow "infringe" on some turf carved out by another department or college.

This system means that professors of economics who know almost nothing about accounting, have the same vote on approval of accounting curriculum matters as do professors of accounting. At the university level, economics professors will vote on physics courses. Consider an analogy. Do hospitals make pediatricians get approval from oncologists before changing their methods of providing pediatric services? Of course not, yet that is essentially what colleges do. It is in the current interests of the faculty, as a group, to be able to block changes that other faculty may propose that could change the status quo, such as design an attractive program that may draw students away from existing programs. The lengthy, multistep internal review procedure substantially increases the cost of trying to implement change or even just to provide better information about the actual content of a course. Innovation is stifled by internal barriers to change that do not serve to protect quality.

In response to this allegation, defenders of the status quo claim that the purpose of "democratic" decision making is to ensure curriculum quality. That is nonsense; faculty have little expertise outside their own area. Defenders also argue that the rule makes little difference in practice because the faculty approve most proposed curriculum changes anyway. But that tells us little because faculty read the political tea leaves and do not waste time preparing paperwork and attending committee meetings for proposals that they think will fail. Professors have adjusted their behavior to account for the structure in which they operate. Skills do not evolve in this system, although they might in colleges where faculty have more freedom to determine curriculum and are rewarded for innovations.

Status Quo Standoff

The political situation created by committee-based decision making means departments are hostage to each other, and faculty are hostage to each other. That is, accounting usually gets what it wants by implicit deals with marketing. Neither department is likely to break such deals. No department will threaten another by suggesting radical changes in curriculum, such as dropping marketing requirements for accounting majors. Because the status quo was flawed from the start, it is not likely to improve. Time decays whatever logic there may have been in the degree programs crafted decades ago.

Several years ago we saw a business school "redesign" its MBA program. The committee was told to put the whole program on the table—nothing was sacred. After months of meetings, the new program looked like the old one, but some new labels were put on the not-so-fine same old wine. All five departments in the business college were represented on the committee. The MBA degree had a thirty-hour minimum core requirement consisting of, guess what, six hours taught by each of the five departments, just as before.

Lip service was given to the problem that plagues most MBA programs—not having sufficient communication skills components—but that would have meant including nonbusiness college faculty who were capable of doing professional communication instruction. Because that change would have cost the business college credit hours or at least directed resources to a department other than the status quo represented on the committee, they avoided a useful change that everyone knew was needed. The committee made vague statements such as, "All faculty will be encouraged to have a writing component in their courses," but no concrete steps were taken. One could have predicted the results of such democratic decision making, but without the umpteen hours devoted to meetings supposedly meant to design a state-of-the-art MBA program. When production decisions are made by existing, well-protected employees, quality is not the issue; what the market wants is not the issue; and what students want is not the issue. Like other self-interested humans, faculty only want to make their lives easier, a goal they can further by cooperating in general turf protection.

More generally, this issue arises in universities that make it difficult to obtain general studies degrees or do not offer them. Such degrees are attractive to students who have no strong interest in any particular degree program and might want an eclectic education. Faculty generally oppose general study programs because it is in the faculty's interest to require students to declare a major and thereby to take a list of required courses that protect the teaching interests of established faculty. The idea that students might shop around for courses of interest is abhorrent to faculty because it means they and their departments must compete with one another to satisfy students' interests.

It is difficult to separate faculty self-interest from courses and program structure. If the status quo is maintained, faculty do not have to tool-up for new courses and do not have to worry as much about losing market share. No one talks in these terms; discussion is politely couched in terms of benefiting the students. No doubt most faculty believe the positions they take, but that is because it is in our self-interest to fight for what benefits us and to cooperate with those who have demonstrated that they will cooperate.

Minifiefdoms

Programs in departments and colleges are like cartels. The members of the cartel, established faculty, carve up the student market and, by the committee decision process, implicitly promise to stick together so that no one can grab a larger market share by offering more of what students want or need. Junior faculty, who are more likely to have fresh ideas than the old guard, had best defer to their senior brethren, who control their chances for promotion and tenure. When junior faculty have voting rights on curriculum matters, it is common for them to watch how the senior faculty in their departments vote. After all, academic freedom should go only so far!

Current university rules generally retard innovation and protect the status quo. What is included in the status quo has grown over time. Required courses are a major faculty entitlement. Equilibrium in degree programs is reached via the voting rules. The major interest of departments is not to work to improve offerings, but to think about how to protect current requirements and how to tack on more required courses. This resource grab is not necessarily related to what is "best." It is best just for the winning majority voting bloc of faculty. The question is, then, how can the status quo be broken so as not to threaten most voters? How can incentives be given so that faculty want to focus on making better course and program innovations?

The status quo defenders' response to this assertion that the committee structure within most colleges inhibits potentially beneficial changes is that this structure ensures that there is no "race to the bottom." That is, vigilant faculty from other departments will block the efforts of a department that wants to give away degrees with no standards. In truth, every university has a department that is the academic basement for the weakest students. Football and basketball players tend to be concentrated in a few degree programs. That aside, there are two valid concerns here. One is that a department must be constrained from making students take too many courses within that department. An economics faculty might guarantee itself more student credit hours (revenues) by requiring that its majors take 45 instead of 30 hours of economics. Imposing such requirements is hard to do if there is oversight of such developments. Second, many students do not know what they want and prefer to avoid work. Too many, left to their own devices, would foolishly skip all substantive courses.

Edicts from the top do not produce good work. Ordering professors to work hard and teach students well does not produce quality education. The cost of monitoring performance is high, and when a product is mostly intellectual, monitoring is difficult. Is someone sitting at his desk staring at a computer thinking about important matters or about vacation? A university is too big to be managed by constant monitoring. Moreover, in a nonprofit, state institution with tenure, edicts can be ignored with few consequences. Faculty need more incentives to perform well.

Constrained Competition

How can the effects of these conflicting forces be reduced? It is unlikely that changes will come about unless external changes are made regarding the way universities are funded, a subject we consider in chapter 8. If we want to encourage competition among faculty and departments so that they focus more on developments intended to serve students, binding decisions by faculty committees must largely be ended. It is the senior administrators and trustees' job, with input from faculty, to declare what common classes should be required of all students at a particular college; such as 12 hours of English, 12 hours of math, 12 hours of science, and so forth. Unless a college has a mission that is different from most, no one department could tell students to come play around for four years and get a degree with no math or science requirement.

Similarly, trustees and administrators should determine if more than 120 semester hours of coursework is justifiable for any degree. In some fields today, such as accounting, higher credit-hour requirements are unavoidable owing to national certification standards. However, many degree programs have expanded for no reasons other than mandatory internal requirements that guarantee to various university interests a slice of the student pie. Similarly, within colleges, the deans should have final control, subject to review upstairs, over what may be allowed or not allowed, but departments should not have to get permission from faculty of other departments to redesign their programs.

Within departments, regular faculty should not have to get permission from their peers to redesign the classes they routinely teach. Proposed changes should be announced so that comments may be made, but only a department head or dean, not faculty from other departments, should be able to stop these changes. Similarly, groups of faculty should be able to get together to design alternative tracks within degree programs or to create new degree programs, without having to get permission from their peers. Suppose some biology and economics faculty designed a new program in bioeconomics that required 15 hours of both biology and economics, not 30 hours of economics or 30 hours of biology. Subject to rejection by the dean for budget reasons, there is no reason the program should be subject to control by faculty from chemistry, history, and art. Deans and other administrators have no special insights into what should be taught in any particular program, but they do have to balance budgets, so they must consider resource reallocation.

Freedom to offer revised courses and programs would reduce decision making based on committee logrolling considerations. Faculty could focus on intellectual curiosity or on a simple effort to be more appealing to students, rather than spend time pondering how to manipulate status quo politics. Nothing in this suggestion means that standards would be reduced.

Some readers may object, correctly, that many disciplines require a uniform structure. Chemical engineering degree programs must have a fixed list of courses in math, engineering, chemistry, and so forth to produce a chemical engineer. That is fine; objective criteria can easily determine whether a chemical engineer has been produced or not. That situation is quite different from fields such as English, economics, liberal arts, and social sciences, where, except for a few general requirements, reasonable people may design very different degree programs. In these cases, maximum flexibility in degree design should be allowed.

Let a Thousand Flowers Bloom

Colleges and departments within universities should have more flexibility to try different things. If the trustees of one college want to have no math requirements for graduation, that is their own and their students' business. The market rewards and punishes; it will penalize colleges that behave foolishly. No central planner can do better by mandating a curriculum for all colleges. This is where trustees and administrators have a duty to decide what the mission of a college is. If they agree that anything goes and there are no requirements, then they should let prospective students and their parents be so informed. If they wish to have a common set of courses required for graduation, or even a completely inflexible curriculum, that should be fine. Diversity across universities will produce, on average, superior results. Different educational models work for different students based on their interests and abilities.

It is the administrators and trustees' duty to stick to the mission of a college by prohibiting courses and other activities that do not meet that mission. That the president of Xavier University in Cincinnati, a Catholic school, thinks it consistent with academic freedom to allow the performance of *The Vagina Monologues,* even though he had "concerns" about the language and themes of the play, is a typical indication of the loss of understanding that administrators can enforce the values defined for a particular university (Postel 2003). This task is no different than monitoring a professor who is supposed to be teaching mathematical economics but in fact just yaks about personal beliefs regarding economic policy. Faculty who do not maintain a worthwhile curriculum should be dismissed; tenure does not protect shirking duties.

Trustees and administrators have final say on what is allowed. Administrators must be rewarded for enforcing rules, such as that faculty must do a competent job of teaching or they will be fired. Faculty presently can shirk their duties to an amazing degree before they get in "trouble" because administrators have little incentive to do what one would expect administrators to do. Disciplinary authority exists, but, as discussed earlier, there is little incentive to use it because it means lowering the boom on lazy faculty, which is a threat to other faculty who worry that they might be next.

A benevolent dictator can maybe micromanage something as small as a department, but not a university. John Silber may have been the most gutsy university president in the country, but after more than two decades at Boston University he could not correct all its ills. The idea that the "right person" can fix all the problems at a college is as silly as thinking that the U.S. president "runs the country." For colleges to perform better, faculty (and administrators) need incentives to think about issues besides carving up the existing pie.

Authority Based on Expertise

The "empowerment" notion has been much discussed in management circles. In colleges, it means giving faculty more authority over their "teaching property." Because the most important asset of faculty is intellectual property, the focus must be on incentives to use and improve that property to the benefit of students and other university clients. Just as hospital oncologists determine most matters regarding cancer treatment, faculty should have substantial latitude over what they teach in their areas of expertise.

Faculty members should publish clear descriptions of their courses. This process should not involve getting permission from their colleagues—a marketing professor should not vote on what is taught in managerial accounting. Of course, just as hospital administrators should be able to prevent an individual oncologist from giving coffee enemas to cure colon cancer, deans and provosts should have veto authority to stop behavior that violates professional norms. Faculty members should have more freedom than most in practice do now to offer courses that are described honestly and are consistent with the college mission.

Instructors should be required, however, to advertise the content of their courses truthfully, even if the college has no clear mission. Under the current rules of the game, at most universities instructors can do pretty much what they please within vague guidelines of what their courses are supposed to be about. They have little incentive to advertise truthfully about what they teach. Because many courses are required, instructors have captive audiences—if a student wants a degree in psychology, she must take a list of specific courses in psychology, as well as a number of other prescribed courses. Students have little freedom to take what they might like from faculty who work to attract students. This arrangement subsidizes bad behavior by faculty—lazy teaching practices and, if the inclination exists, spouting of political or other personal preferences that are only tangentially related to the course subject. This is a major reason why we get many of the horror stories about political correctness, such as the tenured professor in an introductory psychology course at a state college in California who used the forum to attack conventional sex, men, and childbirth. This incident attracted attention only because a student trapped in the course filed a sexual harassment suit against the instructor and the university. The point is not that a professor may teach something peculiar, which is not uncommon, but that students have little choice but to put up with such nonsensical or offensive material because a course is required or was described vaguely or untruthfully. The amount of peculiar material foisted in the classroom might well decline if faculty were to teach exactly what they advertise in their course descriptions.

Core Curriculum or Institutionalized Craziness?

The concern that conservatives express about the lack of a core curriculum in the liberal arts and humanities fails to recognize that the courses they want to force students to take, such as "Western Civilization," may well be taught from a Marxist perspective. Such a course is hardly what these traditionalists have in mind. Even if you have the authority to order extremist faculty to teach what you want taught, the desired results will not occur just because you have issued marching orders. Radical professors may spend the semester mocking the great works they have been ordered to use, which is more destructive than if they had been allowed to do whatever they otherwise would have done. Bizarre classroom performance is just another symptom of the perverse effects of a skewed incentive system for faculty.

To minimize the practice of forcing students to suffer through indoctrination and to put up with truly horrible teachers, we recommend that, in big state universities with no real mission, core curriculums be abolished except in broad terms of so many hours of courses in general areas being required. We have no desire to drive radicals from the academy; we seek only to ensure that students have accurate information about the content of courses and that they be allowed to choose among a wide offering.

This change does not mean that because most students come from traditional backgrounds, they will avoid radical instructors (of any stripe). Many are intrigued by radical approaches. But students have the right to know, before they go into politicized courses, if the professor expects a party line to be followed or if he or she respects other views. Such information would be revealed in reviews from past students, which give not only the marks students give to instructors, but also their written comments, which are often most revealing of all.

Transparency

All courses should be subject to mandatory, substantive student evaluations that are published. Evaluations are only *one* bit of information, of course. They are not always correct, but nothing is wrong with a little public embarrassment for poorly performing teachers.[17] We are all aware that student "opinion may be flawed by lack of experience and long-term perspective and by the pursuit of the pleasure principle" (Rosovsky 1990, 91). However, faculty and students tend to agree in most cases; both can identify the louts in the classroom. There are a few cases of students not fully appreciating good professors or of professional colleagues disliking good professors for personal or political, not academically substantive, reasons. Those matters are for administrators to handle.

Bust Grade Inflation: Help Good Students

Grade inflation has been rising steadily for years, thereby making the informational content of a student transcript less reflective of relative ability (see www.gradeinflation.com). The problem of grade inflation is national, but it is worse at some schools, such as the University of Texas, Austin, and is generally worse at private schools than at public schools (Young 2003).

One way to deal with the problem of grade inflation is to report a grade distribution and the class average grade point average (GPA) with each individual student grade. If each grade in each class can be compared to the class average, and perhaps the department and college average, then the relative difficulty of a particular course will be understood, as will the relative ranking of the student in each course. The relative rank provides more information than the GPA. Instructors who try to buy favor with students by passing out mostly A's will earn fewer "rewards" from students because that fact would be noted on the transcript. An A in a course in which the *class* GPA is 3.80 on a 4.0 scale is much less respectable than a B in a class in which the class GPA is 2.25. Employers and graduate schools are capable of reading such transcripts. Students who take the easiest route through universities are not rewarded at the other end; more information about grades will encourage students to take what is of the most interest and use, rather than discourage them from taking tough but effective Professor So-and-So.

Such moves have been discussed, but not implemented, at some institutions. Duke University's faculty Arts and Sciences Council defeated, nineteen to fourteen, a proposal by a statistics professor to add an "achievement index" to the regular grade (Gose 1997b, A53). The index would take into account the relative difficulty of the class, the toughness of the competition within the class, and so forth. Hence, a C in some courses would be recognized as a greater achievement than an A in other classes. As one would suspect, faculty from the more difficult disciplines supported the proposal, whereas most social science and humanities faculty voted against it. A professor of art history said that the reason students in some other professors' classes do not all get A's is because those professors "cannot elicit excellent work from our excellent students" (Gose 1997a, A47). Such changes in grading policy would help end grade inflation (such as at Duke, where the average GPA is 3.3). It is interesting that this proposal, and ones being considered at other colleges, came from the faculty—not from trustees who have a duty to be concerned about the degradation of grading standards.

Ask Satisfied Customers

Rather than wait to see if graduates liked a college as measured by gifts to the alumni association in later years, colleges might do exit interviews of graduating students (and perhaps of students who flunk out or do not return for other reasons) to see what they think after the fact. When the pressure of immediate grades is past, students tend to be pretty fair-minded about evaluations. They usually report that most faculty were pretty good, but may recall the real duds and praise the few stars. When enough recall a few faculty as losers, that general opinion should become a significant part of the record of a professor's performance.

8

External Reforms

A private college must improve itself by taking initiatives within the institution that the board believes necessary to make the college more successful over time, given its mission. Public colleges, besides instituting internal reforms, can have conditions imposed by the legislature to enhance effectiveness in the higher education market. While most public college presidents assert that an increase in state funding for colleges is the way to improve higher education, throwing more taxpayer money at faulty institutions rarely yields good returns. Legislation that will improve higher education means releasing some controls. Central planning of the details of higher education, no matter how well intended, cannot produce results superior to what will emerge if producers are allowed to compete more to service the college student market.

Post-Tenure Review

Since a key focus of this volume is tenure, this discussion of external reforms begins with mandatory tenure review. A number of state legislatures have mandated periodic review of tenured professors or have cowed boards of regents into adopting such a process. The point is, of course, to force a formal review of tenured professors every so many years so that the bad ones would shape up or be shipped out.

This is not a very useful idea. As noted earlier, the law of tenure already allows for dismissal of incompetent faculty. There is no legal barrier to dismissal for cause. As we have discussed, however, as things stand now, it is generally in the university administrators' best interests not to go after incompetent faculty. There are high costs and few rewards. Requiring tenure review—done by the same faculty and administrators who *already* review faculty performance—means more guarding of the henhouse by the same foxes. There is little reason to expect substantive changes, only a more bureaucratic paperwork, committee work, and hand waving in the name of post-tenure review.

The results in practice have been just that. According to a lawyer at the AAUP, the dismissal of a professor at Kansas State University based on a post-tenure review process was the only instance of that process taking place of which she was aware, despite the fact that thirty-seven states have some form of post-tenure review (Wilson 2002, A10). So let us consider some measures that might help push universities to face more competition, which in turn will help discipline boards, administrators, and faculty so that they are more respectful of their duties.

1. Eliminate Centralized University Systems and State Boards

Every state university should have its own board of trustees and should stand alone. University systems, which may have one board over the entire system, exist primarily for the benefit of the flagship of the system, such as Chapel Hill in the University of North Carolina system and Austin in the University of Texas system. Other campuses in the system are under the thumb of centralized system personnel, who usually hail from and are loyal to the flagship. The flagship campuses have enough going for them already without the power to restrict competition from other colleges in the system. System boards of trustees tend to be dominated by people most loyal to the flagship because it is usually the oldest, largest, and most successful campus and has turned out generations of lawyers and business executives who, when appointed to the board, naturally think mostly about the flagship school, as do system administrators. The flagship school also produces big events such as bowl games, trips to the NCAA basketball tournaments, and visits by celebrities—all of which trustees and political leaders value as perks.

In many states, even if there is no university system, state commissions or boards of higher education work to monopolize the production of public university education. Each state college must go through a lengthy and costly process to get permission to offer various degrees and programs. The time costs in preparing the information demanded by commissions to justify a new program can mean that a college must wait years to institute a program that students, faculty, and employers want and perhaps need now. Innovation is discouraged. There are few rewards for productive people for writing program justifications and for pasting together reams of tedious boilerplate needed in presentations to bureaucrats in state capitals. This is the opposite of a public policy that would promote quality programs for the diverse interests of the students and for related constituent groups served by colleges.

Contrary to the asserted justifications for centralized control, administrators at competing universities have no incentive to duplicate what is found on other campuses, unless the state funding formula provides such incentives. Colleges have incentives not only to consider successful programs, but also to develop unique programs aimed at drawing students from other institutions. Revenues follow students to college campuses, thereby rewarding successful offerings. Commissions and central boards block some programs because they presume that somehow they, sitting in the state capital, have far more wisdom than do trustees, faculty, and administrators at numerous universities who are on the front lines interacting with students and employers.

As is often the case with regulatory agencies, former politicians or their cronies have ended up in control of statewide university boards. Who, after all, knows better how to work their way around the capital than a former legislator? But no one asserts that politicians have great leadership insights in higher education. Public colleges become increasingly political the more control is centralized and the more colleges must rely on legislative largess for appropriations.

Like other bureaucracies, higher education commissions and boards are political and must be responsive to petitioners with political clout. If a college can get the governor or a key legislator to press for what it wants, that college is much more likely to get the funding than all the academic merit in the world. The less college heads have to play political games to get this or that, however, and the more they can concentrate on trying to offer successful programs, the better the students and taxpayers will be. Commissions force state colleges to think in terms of what will win political support, not what they think is needed. Some utterly worthless programs have been requested and funded simply because university leaders knew the programs would fly with the central bureaucracy—usually because a favor is being done for some legislator. That's how governments work whether it is highway construction or higher education funding. But even if university commissions could magically be divorced from politics, they still cannot plan higher education better than can independent universities competing with each other to offer successful programs.

Moving away from state systems and other forms of central control is not easy.[18] Governor Mitt Romney of Massachusetts stirred up a hornet's nest in 2003, when, as part of an effort to balance the state's budget, he proposed breaking up the centralized state university system (Selingo 2003). Getting rid of the central office itself, which contains the president of the system (a former state senator), would save $14 million a year. The governor proposed making the flagship campus, at Amherst, independent to set its own tuition and be more aggressive in the national market. He also proposed gradually privatizing the state's medical school and two other colleges and merging a couple of small, low-enrollment schools. The attempt to shake up the system met, of course, with opposition from the colleges and members of the legislature who saw their special interest threatened.

Eliminating systems would reverse a trend that started around thirty years ago. At the time, this allegedly "progressive" move promised to prevent program duplication and to lower administrative costs. But central administrators can no more efficiently control universities than Congress can plan optimal university structure for all states. At a time when there is growing recognition that over-centralization of one-size-fits-all K-12 education is not effective (Merrifield 2003), some states are making the same mistake in public higher education by moving to greater central planning and control.

A few states have gone the other way. In an effort to save some money, Governor Christie Whitman of New Jersey abolished the state's Board of Higher Education in 1994. Although her primary motivation in this case was to cut state spending, there are even better reasons for abolishing such commissions. The New Jersey board, which had three hundred employees (enough to staff a small college), regulated state colleges and controlled much of the budgetary process. Each college had its own trustees, but they were approved by the board and the governor. The head of the board was a trustee at every college. The board justified itself "as the bastion of institutional accountability" (Greer and Shelly 1995, 17). Although that may have been so, no one ever accused New Jersey of having a distinguished public college system; a higher percentage of New Jersey students leave the state to go to college than do students from any other state.

The board was replaced by the New Jersey Presidents Council, which is supposed to encourage cooperation among state schools, and by a small, nonregulatory central staff. Central regulations and controls were eliminated. Each college board controls personnel policies, has final say on internal academic matters, sets tuition and fees, retains legal counsel, and controls college planning and accountability. Like Ohio and Virginia, New Jersey now has one of the most decentralized college systems in the United States.

The trustees of a university system, even if they meet monthly, can hardly gain expertise about the problems of different institutions scattered around the state. There will be more genuine oversight if each campus has one board composed of loyal alumni and local leaders. Such boards will spend more time learning and thinking about what is happening at their campuses than will a remote board that relies for information from central administration bureaucrats who work energetically to expand their own powers and budgets. The board can help a president manage, and a board is key to generating extra financial resources. Most boards are local in flavor, so they can bring the business community in to help support a college that is on the right track and can make sure that the college sticks to the mission that the community thinks most appropriate for it.

In 1982, two famous management books were published, John Naisbitt's *Megatrends* and Thomas Peters and Robert Waterman's *In Search of Excellence*. Both books attacked central planning and its obsession with costs as the measure of input control, rather than with quality of output. Following their ideas, Wade Gilley, Kenneth Fulmer, and Sally Reithling published *Searching for Academic Excellence* in 1986. They concluded that state central planning of higher education was not working. "In the 20 institutions we visited, there was not one instance of a state coordinating board level initiative that improved quality; promoted efficiency; addressed a major societal or educational issue; encouraged an institution to seek new levels of excellence; or anticipated trends or issues. Instead, we discovered that in the public institutions, state coordination agencies constituted on the most significant obstacles to innovation and change" (1986, 11).

As we learned from the collapse of the USSR, state-controlled production does not work even in "simple" things such as growing wheat; it works even less well in the control of highly complex institutions, such as universities. Critics of the market process have complained that it means "making things without permission." But that is exactly *why* markets produce what people want. Consider the alternative. If one must seek official permission to produce something—whether that be a software program or a new degree in crime scene investigation—that process implies that the person from whom permission is being sought knows more about the production process and the market than do the people forced to seek permission. There is no evidence from state governing commissions that such all-knowing central decision makers exist.

In the absence of central commissions, colleges make their annual budget requests to the appropriate committees in the legislature. Elected representatives decide how tax dollars will be allocated for higher education. While we think this is superior to having a state commission that serves as an added layer of bureaucracy and politics in spending decisions, reform can be taken to a higher level. The legislature can eliminate much of the appropriation process and decide how much to grant students for tuition support. We discuss such options in the next sections.

2. Allow State Universities to Set Tuition

Most state legislatures either set university tuition directly or assign this task to a central bureaucracy. In most states, the tuition is the same whether an in-state student attends a world-class institution such as the University of California, Berkeley or a less-distinguished school such as the University of California, Santa Cruz. The fact that the flagship institution has the same price as the lesser universities is further evidence of how the systems are rigged to benefit the flagships. The lead institution gets to offer what is perceived as the "best" education in the state system at the same price one must pay for "lesser" education at the "component" institutions. Furthermore, on average, students from wealthier families attend flagship institutions, so there is an implicit subsidy running from the parent-taxpayer who sends a child to Santa Cruz to the parent-taxpayer who sends a child to Berkeley.

Recent budget crunches in the states have helped force moves to tuition reform. In 2003, the Texas legislature voted to move toward allowing individual state universities to set their tuitions at different levels. This was a practical way of letting state schools bring in revenues they claim they must have to survive. The most popular universities, Texas A&M and the University of Texas, Austin, can be expected to raise their tuition the most. While this has generated yowls of protest, it will allow the less-popular universities in the state to discriminate on the basis of price as a way of attracting more students and, thereby, having a chance to improve their fortunes over time.

3. Institute a "GI Bill" for All Students

Rather than make direct appropriations to universities based on credit hours or some other formula, states could give every in-state student eligible for admission to an accredited university a voucher for an amount equal to the sum currently allocated to universities by the tuition formula plus assorted line items in the budget.

If that amount is equal to $250 per credit hour, or $3,750 for a 15-hour semester, the college is credited with that sum when a student enrolls, up to 120 credit hours. Some states have limits on the number of credits a student can take at the in-state tuition rate. Such rules discourage students from spending too much time hanging around trying to decide what to do, at taxpayer expense. Obviously, like now, weaker students will not be admitted to the premier universities, but there will be some place for everyone, and the schools will compete more to attract students than they do now. The cost to taxpayers will be about the same, but students and their parents, not lobbied legislators, will determine which colleges are doing the best job of offering programs of interest. There will thus be more diversity in program offerings than we see now.

As long as state colleges rely on legislatures for their budgets, like any bureaucracy they will spend great effort fighting for larger budgets. There is less incentive to do a good job with the resources at hand, such as getting rid of incompetent professors, and more incentive to lobby for programs that may be politically attractive but are of dubious value. If students carry tuition grants with them, colleges will work harder to satisfy them. This system also eliminates the worry about "needless" duplication. The programs that students value will survive, and others will be created.

Public colleges suffer from booms and busts owing to fluctuations in state revenues and the favor in which the colleges themselves are held at any particular time. For example, over the two years from 1994 to 1996, state support for higher education rose 20 percent in some states (Nevada and California), while it was falling 10 percent in New York ("Trusteeship" 1996, 2). These kinds of budget swings make little sense and greatly reduce administrators' ability to plan sensibly. Enrollment and voucher support, in contrast, are unlikely to rise or fall by such large percentages in short times, allowing better long-term planning.

We want colleges to compete for students so that they have incentives to offer good value for the money (as judged by students, their parents, and others who care about the quality of colleges). Private colleges compete fiercely for students. Public colleges compete less intensely. With greater competition among public colleges, we would see more variation in what they do, just as we see it among private colleges. There would be much more diversity among the structure of public colleges. Diversity would not mean certain numbers of students of various races, but rather differences in university missions. Undergraduate teaching institutions would have much more incentive to stick to their knitting, just as quality private liberal arts colleges focus on their own individual missions.

The best model we have for generating this voucher system is the GI Bill. During World War II, Congress debated many measures that would provide educational benefits to service personnel after the war. The GI Bill gave qualified students the ability to transport their tuition payments to the college of their choice. It was a straightforward system: the GIs would attend a university of their choosing (that would accept them) anywhere in the country, and the tuition monies would follow them. The history of this system is instructive on several counts.

AN "UNWORKABLE" SYSTEM

There was little controversy over giving educational benefits to veterans. Instead, the debate was over the form the benefits would take. When the GI Bill was discussed in Congress, the American Council on Education, representing public and private colleges, lobbied for financial support directly to colleges. The colleges argued that they needed resources to expand so that they could handle the influx of new students, but they wanted direct appropriation rather than a system in which the GIs would be allowed to choose any college and thereby carry the public funding with them.

James Conant, the president of Harvard at the time, attacked the GIs' ability to go to school anywhere they were admitted: "In education . . . we must guard the doctrine of local responsibility." The president of Chicago, Robert Hutchins, agreed: "It is not merely reckless, it is an open invitation to any entrepreneur of the proper political persuasion in a given state to buy up the charters of a dozen bankrupt colleges and make his fortune" (Conant and Hutchins quoted in Bennett 1994, 11). Conant found the bill, as passed, to be "distressing" because "we may find the least capable among the war generation . . . flooding the facilities for advanced education." He wanted a program that would support only "a carefully selected number of returned veterans" (quoted in Olson 1994, 22). Hutchins attacked the bill as "unworkable" and predicted that the vets would flock to low-quality colleges that would admit and retain unqualified vets in order to collect the money.

No such thing happened. The students were serious and did

not fritter away the opportunity by going to sham colleges. Most GIs went to public colleges, but some went to church-related schools. Quota systems that restricted the number of positions for Jewish and Catholic students at some schools were overturned as they competed for students. "The impetus came ... not from the top ... but from freedom of choice—and the ability to pay for it" (Bennett 1994, 11).

Without the choice provided by the GI Bill, many blacks would not have had opportunities newly opened to them. Most blacks lived in segregated states; if the states were allowed to control the funds, blacks would not have been allowed to attend quality state institutions and thus would have been forced to attend low-quality black colleges in the South—whose funding was also controlled by the states that sought control of these new federal funds. The GI Bill allowed students to go wherever they were qualified—and to take their support to black colleges if they so desired. Indeed, black colleges benefited more than white colleges. But northern colleges also competed for qualified black students, which opened opportunities for graduate education that did not exist in the South (Wilson 1994, 32).

The desire of established colleges to protect the existing order failed. Congress passed the GI Bill under the slogan "This is a bill for veterans, not for educators" (Bennett 1994, 11). Because the bill allowed open competition for students, new schools, such as Antioch College, got their foot in the door and benefited by attracting GIs. Antioch was one of the first colleges to start a cooperative education program. This program would have made Antioch ineligible for GI Bill benefits under the criteria proposed by the American Council on Education, which was not interested in deviations from the established norm.

As would be expected, the wave of new students competed to get in the best schools. Of the 2.2 million who attended college under the bill, 41 percent registered at thirty-eight colleges. Wisconsin's enrollment jumped from 11,400 to 18,700; Stanford's from 4,800 to 7,200. After the fact, it was recognized that the vets *raised* the average student quality, largely because of their seriousness. Clark Kerr, president emeritus of the University of California, said "Subsidized students were less likely to be subject to government controls than subsidized institutions, and students could make better and quicker choices in the market among institutions and their programs than could slower moving bureaucracies in distant offices" (1994, 31).

Peter Drucker says that the GI Bill "signaled the shift to the knowledge society" and may have been "the most important event of the 20th century" (1993, 3). What Drucker is referring to is the beginning of an era in which a large share of America's working population became college educated. The GI Bill showed us how well a college finance system can work that allows students to carry their publicly subsidized tuition support with them, rather than having public support go directly to colleges, which then offer subsidized services to students.

It is unlikely that if existing colleges had their way in 1944—more legislative largess for the status quo—the results would have been as favorable. If enough money is thrown at anything, there can be results. The genius of the GI Bill was that it forced colleges to compete a little bit harder for students who rewarded the college chosen with their dollars. Federal Pell grants and similar loan programs have somewhat the same effect as the GI Bill because students can carry their loans to any college that accepts them.

Today most financial support for undergraduate higher education is at the state level. States should replicate the essential wisdom of the GI Bill, giving students more leverage as consumers of higher education. The result will be better educational services for every tax dollar devoted to higher education. Students could have the right to take their "voucher" to a private school or (even more disturbing to legislators) to schools in other states. This proposal, which is hardly radical, will scare many legislators and higher education leaders, just as the GI Bill scared some college presidents who predicted that it would be a disaster. The status quo is always more comfortable; competition is tough.

4. Decide if the State Wants to Subsidize Graduate Education

Around forty years ago, states were concerned about the relative scarcity of Ph.D.s and other graduate degrees. The race to subsidize graduate education was on. The heavy subsidy provided to people like us when we were graduate students means that today there are plenty of underemployed Ph.D.s around. As long as legislatures funnel cash to such graduate programs, which in some states get as much as ten times the level of formula funding as do undergraduate student credit hours, universities will happily produce unneeded graduate degrees. Legislators who wish to reduce colleges' incentives to produce graduate degrees can easily change the funding formula. They could reward undergraduate enrollment. If states wish to "fine-tune" degree production, they can offer bonuses for students who are qualified to be in graduate programs in fields where there is a market for more graduates, such as computer systems engineering.

Why should taxpayers pay to educate people who, because of their graduate education, expect to earn above average incomes? Because graduates are mobile, taxpayers in Minnesota may pay to educate a Ph.D. who goes to work in Florida. Ph.D.s in history are pretty inexpensive to produce (there is a glut of them, but states continue to subsidize their production), but M.D.s and Ph.D.s in technical areas are expensive to produce. The state of Texas estimates that it "spends about $283,000 for each student graduating from one of its seven public medical schools ... and about $300,000 more on students during a typical primary-care residency" ("Texas' Prescription" 1996, T4).

Rather than pay universities directly for their graduate programs, legislatures could offer a voucher program for qualified students who want to attend graduate school. A legislature would have to decide how many vouchers to offer and if the vouchers will be loans or grants. Grants could become loans to be repaid if a student left the state after graduation. Most state universities have too many graduate programs, and some universities that currently have graduate programs should not have them at all. Many universities would not have such programs if the legislatures did not reward them for churning out relatively low-quality Ph.D.s for which there is little demand.

Perhaps taxpayer support should be withdrawn (no vouchers provided) from many state graduate programs. States have no reason to subsidize law schools; there are buckets of lawyers around, and law schools are nothing more than cash cows for universities. Law schools in state universities, as is the case with graduate schools of business, should be required to make it on their own, charging full fare, as do their private competitors. Given that law and business graduates expect to earn incomes substantially above average, there is no justification for having taxpayers subsidize their education.

Despite the large sums states have invested in expensive graduate programs, the best graduate programs are, with a few exceptions, at private universities and at a few elite public schools. If such programs are worthwhile at state universities, then universities will be able to compete by charging higher tuition. The argument that graduate programs should be subsidized because they attract industry to the area is as dubious as the claim that professional sports teams and stadiums should be subsidized in order to attract industry.[19]

9

Conclusion

Higher education in America is the best in the world. Unlike our high schools, which compare poorly to other nations, American higher education puts Japan, France, and other countries with respected high school programs to shame. Rosovsky notes that American higher education is great because of competition. "That Harvard and Stanford, for example, actively recruit and compete for students ... is quite incomprehensible to establishments such as Tokyo and Kyoto universities, where an entrance examination determines all" (1987, 13). Similarly, in most countries, universities do not compete for faculty; professors are civil servants of the central government, essentially tenured for life upon being hired (Altbach 2002). Politics, not academic competition, controls who gets what.

A benefit of quality higher education is that higher education is a major service export of the United States. We run a trade surplus in the knowledge business. Quality higher education arose under decentralized management and is a choice system. Other countries compete poorly because their national university systems are run by central bureaucracies in the national capital. As so-called reform in the United States has progressively moved to centralized control of higher education, we have reduced choice, retarded innovation, and gradually undermined quality. State-planned monopolies are not consumer friendly, so it is little wonder that private universities, without the benefit of resources and control from state legislatures, dominate the top end of academic quality.

Adam Smith understood all this more than two centuries ago: "Whatever forces a certain number of students to any college or university, independent of the merit or reputation of the teachers, tends more or less to diminish the necessity of that merit or reputation.... Were the students ... left free to chuse [*sic*] what college they liked best, such liberty might perhaps contribute to excite some emulation among different colleges" ([1776] 1981, 719).

Critics of higher education have good reason to be disturbed by some of the foolishness observed in colleges, but the focus on tenure is misplaced. That tenure appears to protect incompetent professors is merely a symptom of structural defects that limit competition. "Reforming" tenure without addressing the structural defects will not result in improvements. Instead reform should aim to bring stronger trustee oversight and involvement in universities, more choice for students, more accountability for faculty and administrators, and more competition among our universities by removing many of the bureaucratic constraints they now face. When creative people are allowed and encouraged to compete, wealth and opportunities expand. Our universities can benefit from the wonders of this dynamic process to ensure that the United States will remain the leader in freedom of thought and new learning.

Appendix: Synopsis of Cases Since 1990 in Federal and State Appeals Courts Regarding Tenure

This summary lists cases identified on WestLaw using the key words *tenure, faculty,* and *college* or *university.* It excludes junior or community college cases and cases in which existing faculty claimed discrimination in pay or other working conditions. As the list indicates, most cases are for denial of tenure. Very few cases involve the dismissal of a faculty member for poor performance. There is probably no more litigation resulting from dismissal of college faculty than occurs in other sectors of employment. The courts routinely uphold administrative decisions to fire faculty so long as proper procedure is followed and there is not simple discrimination based on sex, race or other protected class status. Our experience is that college boards and administrators are confused about the legal status of tenure and think that faculty have rights that make them untouchable regardless of performance, but such is not the case. As the book has discussed, the problem is not the law of tenure, or the fact that it exists, but that there is little incentive for administrators to exercise the authority they have to discipline poor performance.

The cases are presented beginning with the most recent, and each case includes the following information:

Case name, legal citation, court, and year
Key facts
Essential basis of suit ("1983 claims" are general claims of violation of constitutional rights, such as freedom of speech or due process)
Disposition of case by court(s)

Federal Courts of Appeal

Case name, legal citation, court, & year	Key facts	Essential basis of suit	Disposition of case by court(s)
Trejo v. Shoben, 319 F.3d 878 (7th Cir., 2003)	Untenured assistant professor of psychology dismissed for bad behavior, University of Illinois-Urbana	Free speech violation (retaliation), due process violations	Summary judgment for university upheld
Llano v. Berglund, 282 F.3d 1031 (8th Cir., 2002)	Tenured physics professor at North Dakota State University terminated for bad behavior and teaching problems	First Amendment, due process	University granted summary judgment; affirmed on appeal
Hedrich v. Board of Regents of U. Wisconsin System, 274 F.3d 1174 (7th Cir., 2001)	Untenured assistant professor of physical education denied tenure at University of Wisconsin-Whitewater	First Amendment, equal protection, due process	District court dismissed suit; affirmed on appeal
Katz v. Georgetown Univ., 246 F.3d 685 (D.C. Cir., 2001)	Tenured medical school professor fired owing to financial crisis at medical school	Claimed procedure was violated; requested injunction requiring one-year notice prior to dismissal	District court refused request; appeals court affirmed
Nicholas v. Pennsylvania State Univ., 227 F.3d 133 (3rd Cir., 2000)	Tenured professor of medicine fired	First Amendment, due process, breach of contract	Summary judgment granted university; remanded to allow revision of complaint on appeal
Alvin v. Zuzuki, 227 F.3d 107 (3rd Cir., 2000)	Tenured professor in pharmacy school at University of Pittsburgh transferred to dental school over his objection	First Amendment (1983), breach of contract	Summary judgment granted university; remanded to allow revision of complaint on appeal

Case name, legal citation, court, & year	Key facts	Essential basis of suit	Disposition of case by court(s)
Weinstock v. Columbia University, 224 F.3d 33 (2d Cir., 2000)	Assistant professor of chemistry denied tenure	Title VII claim	Summary judgment granted for university; affirmed on appeal
Clinger v. New Mexico Highlands Univ., 215 F.3d 1162 (10th Cir., 2000)	Assistant professor of art denied tenure at New Mexico Highlands University	First Amendment (1983), due process, Title VII	District court granted university summary judgment; affirmed on appeal
Lighton v. Univ. of Utah, 209 F.3d 1213 (10th Cir., 2000)	Assistant professor of biology claimed constructive dismissal; he had been accused of having an affair with a student and had moved to the University of Nevada at Las Vegas	First Amendment (1983), due process	District court granted summary judgment to university; appeals court affirmed
Lawrence v. Curators of the Univ. of Missouri, 204 F.3d 807 (8th Cir., 2000)	Assistant professor of accounting denied tenure and promotion	Title VII sex discrimination claim	District court granted university summary judgment; affirmed on appeal
Bickerstaff v. Vassar College, 196 F.3d 435 (2d Cir. 1999)	Female, black associate professor of Africana not promoted to full professor	Title VII, Equal Pay Act	College granted summary judgment; appeals court affirmed
Dobbs-Weinstein v. Vanderbilt Univ., 185 F.3d 542 (6th Cir., 1999)	Assistant professor of philosophy denied tenure	Title VII for gender and national origin discrimination	University granted summary judgment; appeals court affirmed
Feldman v. Ho, 171 F.3d 494 (7th Cir., 1999)	Untenured assistant professor of math at Southern Illinois University did not have his contract renewed after four years	First Amendment and tortuous interference with employment contract	District court held for professor; appeals court reversed for university and department head

Case name, legal citation, court, & year	Key facts	Essential basis of suit	Disposition of case by court(s)
LaForge v. Crowley, 168 F.3d 499 (9th Cir., 1999), unpublished	Contract of untenured assistant professor terminated at University of Nevada, Reno	1983 claim	Dismissed by trial court; affirmed on appeal
Webb v. Board of Trustees of Ball State Univ., 167 F.3d 1146 (7th Cir., 1999)	Two criminology professors claimed retaliation by administration	First Amendment claims	District court denied professors' request for injunction; affirmed on appeal
Williams v. Alabama State Univ., 102 F.3d 1179 (11th Cir., 1997)	Assistant professor of English denied tenure	First Amendment (1983)	District court refused to dismiss case; reversed by appeals court (dismissed)
Bunder v. Univ. of Oklahoma Board of Regents, 95 F.3d 987 (10th Cir., 1996)	Two untenured assistant professors of business did not have contracts renewed at Cameron University	1983 claims	District court granted summary judgment to university; appeals court affirmed
EEOC v. Catholic University of America, 83 F.3d 455 (DC Cir., 1996)	Assistant professor of religion denied tenure	Title VII religion discrimination claim	District court dismissed case; appeals court affirmed
Fisher v. Vassar College, 70 F.3d 1420 (2d cir., 1995)	Professor of biology denied tenure	Title VII claims	District court held for plaintiff; appeals court reversed on most claims
McDaniels v. Flick, 59 F.3d 446 (3rd Cir., 1995)	Business professor at Delaware Community College fired for sexual harassment	1983 claims	District court held for professor; appeals court reversed for college
Jiminez v. Mary Washington College, 57 F.3d 369 (4th Cir., 1995)	Economics professor terminated for failure to get Ph.D., no research, and bad teaching	Title VII race and national origin claims	District court held for professor; appeals court reversed for college

Case name, legal citation, court, & year	Key facts	Essential basis of suit	Disposition of case by court(s)
Mumford v. Godfried, 52 F.3d 756 (8th Cir., 1995)	Assistant professor of architecture at Iowa State University denied tenure	1983 claim and tort of interference with contract	District court dismissed; appeals court affirmed except for one part of speech claim
Bina v. Providence College, 39 F.3d 21 (1st Cir., 1994)	Economics professor denied tenure	Title VII and breach of contract claims	District court granted summary judgment to college; appeals court affirmed
San Filippo v. Bongiovanni, 30 F.3d 424 (3rd Cir., 1994)	Tenured chemistry professor at Rutgers University fired	1983 claims	District court granted summary judgment to university; appeals court held that certain portions of the claim had been improperly dismissed and should be allowed to proceed
Wesley v. Michigan State University, 25 F.3d 1052 (6th Cir., 1994), unpublished	Tenured business professor resigned when punished for sexual harassment	Title VII religion discrimination claim	District court granted university summary judgment; appeals court affirmed
Blum v. Schlegel, 18 F.3d 1005 (2d Cir., 1994)	Law professor denied tenure at SUNY Buffalo	Free speech, property, and due process claims	District court dismissed suit; appeals court affirmed
Yu v. Peterson, 13 F.3d 1413 (10th Cir., 1993)	Tenured professor of engineering fired for plagiarism at University of Utah	1983 claims	District court dismissed case; appeals court affirmed
Feldman v. Bahn, 12 F.3d 730 (7th Cir., 1993)	Untenured math professor at Southern Illinois University did not have contract renewed after he accused a colleague of plagiarism	1983 claims	District court refused to dismiss; appeals court reversed (dismissed)

Case name, legal citation, court, & year	Key facts	Essential basis of suit	Disposition of case by court(s)
Williams v. Texas Tech Univ., 6 F.3d 290 (5th Cir., 1993)	Medical School lowered a professor's salary	Due process claims	District court dismissed; appeals court affirmed
Colburn v. Trustees of Indiana University, 973 F.2d 581 (7th Cir., 1992)	Two sociology professors denied tenure at Indiana University–Purdue University	First and Fourteenth Amendment claims	District court dismissed; appeals court affirmed on appeal
Evans v. Cleveland State Univ. Board of Trustees, 934 F.2d 322 (6th Cir., 1991), unpublished	White male professor of engineering denied tenure at Cleveland State	Title VII claim	Summary judgment at district court for university; affirmed on appeal
Villanueva v. Wellesley College, 930 F.2d 124 (1st Cir., 1991)	Assistant professor of Spanish denied tenure	Title VII claim	District court granted summary judgment to college; appeals court affirmed
Jackson v. Harvard Univ., 900 F.2d 464 (1st Cir., 1990)	Harvard Business School professor denied tenure	Title VII claim	District court found for Harvard; appeals court affirmed
Brown v. Trustees of Boston Univ., 891 F.2d 337 (1st Cir., 1990)	English professor denied tenure	Title VII claim	District court found for plaintiff and ordered that she be given tenure; affirmed in part

State Courts

Case name, legal citation, court, & year	Key facts	Essential basis of suit	Disposition of case by court(s)
Fox v. Parker, 98 SW3d 713 (Ct. App., Tex., 2003)	Baylor University anthropology professor terminated for alleged sexual misconduct	Defamation and breach of contract	District court found for professor on breach of contract; $154,000 damages awarded; both reversed on appeal
Ferrer v. Trustees of Univ. of Penn., 825 A.2d 591 (Sup. Ct., Pa., 2002)	Vet school professor accused of research misconduct	Breach of contract for sanctions imposed after he was found not responsible for research misconduct	Jury awarded professor $5 million; superior court reversed for school; Pennsylvania Supreme Court reinstated jury verdict

Case name, legal citation, court, & year	Key facts	Essential basis of suit	Disposition of case by court(s)
Karle v. Board of Trustees/ Marshall Univ., 575 SE2d 267 (Sup. Ct. App., W.Va., 2002)	Nursing school professor denied tenure	Appeal of state employee's grievance procedure where she claimed due process violations	Circuit court and West Virginia Supreme Court upheld decision of no tenure
Craine v. Trinity College, 791 A.2d 518 (Sup. Ct., Conn., 2002)	Woman chemistry professor denied tenure	Title VII, breach, emotional distress	Jury found for professor on all counts except age discrimination; judge set aside emotional distress; Supreme Court threw out sex discrimination verdict, upheld breach claim owing to college's failure to comply with faculty manual regarding tenure; negligent misrepresentation also upheld owing to bad instructions given professor regarding requirements to achieve tenure
Bentil v. Univ. of Washington, 2002 WL 258033 (App. Div. 1, Wash., 2002), unpublished	Black professor of construction resigned in protest of not being reappointed chair	Title VII, defamation, constructive discharge	Summary judgment for university; affirmed on appeal
Pollock v. Univ. Southern Calif, 2001 WL 1513870 (Ct. App., Calif.), unpublished	Tenured professor of neuroscience fired for neglect of duty and misconduct	Breach of contract and discrimination	Demurrer by university sustained (professor failed to exhaust administrative remedies); affirmed on appeal
Murphy v. Duquesne University, 777 A.2d 418 (Sup. Ct., Pa., 2001)	Tenured professor of law fired for serious misconduct (including sexual harassment)	Breach of contract	Summary judgment for university; affirmed on appeal; affirmed on further appeal

Case name, legal citation, court & year	*Key facts*	*Essential basis of suit*	*Disposition of case by court(s)*
Stanton v. Tulane Univ, 777 So.2d 1242 (Ct. App., La., 2001)	Untenured professor of architecture dismissed for failure to make progress	Breach of contract, tortious interference	Summary judgment against professor; affirmed on appeal
Univ. Nevada, Reno v. Stacey, 997 P.2d 812 (Sup. Ct., Nev., 2000)	Biology professor denied tenure	Breach of contract (he received "excellent" rating and was told that would get him tenure)	District court held for professor; reversed on appeal (the granting of tenure is discretionary)
Roquitte v. Univ. of Minnesota, 2000 WL 249263 (CT. App., Minn.), unpublished	Tenured professor fired for nonperformance	Appealed (per state law in Minnesota)	University decision affirmed
Kirschenbaum v. Northwestern University, 728 N.E.2d 752 (App. Ct. 1st Dist, Ill., 1999)	Professor of medicine granted tenure at zero salary	Breach of contract	District court found for university; affirmed on appeal
Cooper v. Texas Wesleyan Univ, 1999 WL 1179613 (Ct. App., Tx.), unpublished	Law professor denied tenure	Breach of contract for improper procedure	Summary judgment for university; affirmed on appeal
Cherry v. Utah State Univ, 966 P.2d 866 (Ct. App., Utah, 1998)	Contract for untenured assistant professor of dance not renewed	Breach of contract	Summary judgment for university; affirmed on appeal
Univ. of Baltimore v. Iz, 716 A.2d 1107 (Ct. Spcl. App., Mary., 1997)	Professor of business denied tenure	Constitutional claims, breach, and torts	District court found for professor on breach of contract, awarded $425,000 damages; reversed by appeals court
Calif. Faculty Assn v. Superior Court, 75 Cal. Rptr.2d 1 (Ct. App., 6th Dist., Calif., 1998)	Faculty of social science at San Jose State denied tenure	Faculty union sought arbitration; arbitrator overturned university decision	District court overturned arbitrator's decision; appeals court affirmed

Case name, legal citation, court, & year	Key facts	Essential basis of suit	Disposition of case by court(s)
Barazi v. West Va. State College, 498 SE2d 720 (Sup. Ct. App., W.Va., 1997)	Tenured professor of chemistry fired for failure to meet teaching obligations	Breach of contract, due process	District court held that due process was violated; appeals court reversed in part, held damages to $1
Barham v. Univ. Northern Colorado, 964 P.2d 545 (Ct. App., Colo., 1998)	Tenure professor fired for misconduct	Professor sought judicial review of university decision	University decision affirmed
Schwarz v. Administrators of the Tulane Educational Fund, 699 So.2d 895 (Ct. App., La., 1997)	Engineering professor at Tulane University denied tenure	Breach of contract	Summary judgment for university; affirmed on appeal
Long v. Samson, 568 NW2d 602 (Sup. Ct., ND, 1997)	Medical School professor at University of North Dakota denied tenure	Multiple claims	Dismissed by district court; affirmed on appeal
Brewerton v. Dalrymple, 997 SW2d 212 (Sup. Ct., Tx. 1999)	Tenure denied to business professor at University of Texas, Pan American	Emotional distress	District court granted summary judgment to university; Supreme Court affirmed
Marriott v. Cole, 694 A.2d 123 (Ct. Spcl. App., Mary., 1997)	Untenured professor of mental health at Morgan State University fired during tenure track	Constitutional claims and breach of contract	Summary judgment for university; affirmed on appeal
Johns Hopkins Univ. v. Ritter, 689 A.2d 91 (Ct. Spcl. App., Mary., 1997)	Two medical school professors told they were hired with tenure, but were fired after one year	Breach of contract	District court found for plaintiffs; reversed on appeal (must follow university procedure before litigation)
Skimbo v. Eastern Oklahoma State College, 1996 WL 822817 (Ct. App., Ok., 1996)	Tenured professor fired during budget crunch	Breach of contract	Summary judgment for college; affirmed on appeal

Case name, legal citation, court & year	Key facts	Essential basis of suit	Disposition of case by court(s)
Oruma v. Ohio Northern Univ, 1996 WL 492250 (Ct. App. 3rd Dist., Ohio, 1996)	Engineering professor denied tenure	Breach of contract	Dismissed; affirmed on appeal
Taggart v. Drake Univ, 549 NW2d 796 (Sup. Ct., Iowa, 1996)	Professor of art denied tenure	Breach of contract, emotional distress, defamation	Summary judgment for university; affirmed on appeal
Pomona College v. Superior Court, 53 Cal.Rptr.2d 662 (Ct. App., 2d Dist., Calif., 1996)	Language professor denied tenure	Breach of contract	College petitioned for writ of mandate; district court denied; appeals court granted college request
McClellan v. Board of Regents of State University, 921 SW2d 684 (Sup.Ct., Tenn., 1996)	Tenured professor of physical education at Middle Tennessee State punished for sexual harassment	Breach of contract	Complicated lower court proceedings; high court held for university on all counts
Thompson v. Peterson, 546 NW2d 856 (Sup. Ct., ND, 1996)	Untenured history professor at North Dakota State University fired for lack of progress	Breach of contract	District court dismissed; affirmed (must exhaust administrative remedies)
Miller v. Univ. Dayton, 1996 WL 65251 (Ct. App., 2nd Dist., Ohio, 1996)	Management professor denied tenure	Breach of contract	District court held for university; affirmed on appeal
Chan v. Miami University, 652 NE2d 644 (Sup Ct., Ohio, 1995)	Tenured history professor fired for sexual harassment	Breach of contract, due process, Title VII	Supreme Court held for professor for dismissal on improper grounds because the university failed to follow proper procedure
McDowell v. Napolitano, 895 P.2d 218 (Sup. Ct., NW, 1995)	Medical School professor at University of New Mexico denied tenure	1983 claim and breach of contract	District court found for professor on breach, awarded $400,000 damages; affirmed on appeal

Case name, legal citation, court & year	Key facts	Essential basis of suit	Disposition of case by court(s)
Schalow v. Loyola Univ. of New Orleans, 646 So.2d 502 (Ct. App., La., 1994)	Untenured professor fired	Breach of contract	District court found for university; affirmed on appeal
Chronopoulos v. Univ. of Minnesota, 520 NW2d 437 (Ct. App., Minn., 1994)	Tenure denied to computer science professor	Due process and property interest claims	University decision affirmed
McNeill v. New England School of Law, WL 879640 (Super. Ct., Mass.) 1994	Tenured professor of law fired for filing false report	Moved for reinstatement	Injunction denied
Jacobs v. Mundelein College, 628 NE2d 201 (App. Ct., 1st Dist., Ill., 1993)	Untenured English professor fired	Breach of contract and tort claims	District court granted summary judgment to college; affirmed on appeal
Arneson v. Board of Trustees, McKendree College, 569 NE2d 252 (App. Ct., Ill., 1991)	Contract for criminal justice professor not renewed	Breach of contract	District court held for professor; affirmed on appeal (college failed to give professor a terminal year of employment per contract term)
Garner v. Michigan State Univ., 462 NW2d 832 (Ct. App., Mich., 1990)	Tenured professor of psychology fired for allegation of sexual misconduct at previous university	Wrongful discharge	District court ordered reinstatement; affirmed on appeal (university did not follow procedure)
Hom v. State of North Dakota, 459 NW2d 823 (Sup. Ct., ND, 1990)	Dickinson State University professor dismissed during tenure track	Breach of contract	District court found for Dickinson State; reversed on appeal because university did not follow proper procedures

Notes

1. Direct expenditures do not include the income given up by millions of students because they are in school instead of working. For an overview of statistics, see the National Center for Education Statistics at http://nces.ed.gov.

2. This chapter draws on an earlier work sponsored by the Independent Institute. For a more detailed history of the evolution of higher education, see Meiners 1995.

3. Those who harken back to the days when (they think) high-minded scholarship dominated the thoughts of young people attending college should read more about the history of colleges. They have always been places of varying foolishness. In 1842, the *UVA Alumni News* (29 [winter 2000]) reports in that a law professor was killed during one of the late-night student raids called a *calathump,* during which guns were fired, windows were broken, and other drunken merriment took place. Although the death was unusual, destructive, drunken behavior was not—at Virginia and at many other colleges for fine young Christian gentlemen.

4. Veblen, a leading economist of his day, was distressed about the "low" salaries paid to academics, which he found odd given their education. He attributed this situation to the parsimonious nature of the men who ran universities ([1918] 1957, at 117). This kind of sentiment may be why many economists prefer to refer to Veblen as a sociologist.

5. The "Holmes doctrine," or the "rights/privileges distinction," was formalized by then state-court judge Oliver Wendell Holmes in *McAuliffe v. Mayor of New Bedford,* 155 Mass. 216 (1892), where a policeman had been dismissed from the force for engaging in political activities frowned upon by his superiors. There Holmes stated: "The petitioner may have a constitutional right to talk politics, but he has no constitutional right to be a

policeman" (at 220). This doctrine survived until around the mid-1950s; see *Borsky v. Bd. of Regents,* 147 U.S. 442 (1954).

6. In one case, a court found that a college's large-scale discharge of tenured faculty and placement of remaining faculty on short-term contracts, while simultaneously hiring a large number of new faculty, indicated an attempt to abolish its tenure system unilaterally under the guise of financial exigency. The discharges and revisions of employment contracts were reversible owing to the college's bad faith. See *AAUP v. Bloomfield College,* 129 N.J.Super. 249 (1974).

7. K–12 public school teachers have much the same legal status. They are state employees subject to the peculiarities of state law. State employees, including public school teachers, generally have a short probation period, after which they effectively have tenure. They can be dismissed only for cause. That dismissal, as with the dismissal of a tenured professor, requires following proper procedure. In many states, school teachers are unionized, so dismissal is subject to the terms of the collective-bargaining process, which is usually quite protective of the teachers. Even when there are no union procedures to be followed, extensive state-mandated procedure usually discourages dismissal. For example, the Arlington, Texas, school district attorney stated that to dismiss a teacher would run between $60,000 to $150,000 in legal fees and take about six months. She did not know of any contested dismissals in more than five years (Frazier 2003, 1A).

8. As an aside, we ask the reader to think of one highly regarded university that has a unionized faculty. The evidence appears to indicate that the two do not mix, as is also the case for K–12 education (Brimelow 2003).

9. For a number of years, the economics literature discussed the Yugoslavian "worker-managed firm," which has now gone by the boards along with that country. The point was that when workers controlled their place of employment, the results were, as anyone can imagine, miserable.

10. Although most people in higher education pay close attention to assorted rankings of schools, such as those published by *U.S. News,* they dismiss the rankings as not meaningful for a variety of reasons—unless a school comes out pretty well, of course.

11. At one well-known state university, when activist conservatives came to dominate the board, they mandated in the undergraduate curriculum that all students take a year of Western civilization courses. Some faculty members blathered about interference with academic freedom, but soon understood

that the real effect of the decision was to guarantee large enrollments in classes generally taught by people who despise Western civilization—quite the opposite effect of what the trustees intended (or appear to be aware that happened). Such detailed intrusion into curriculum must mean effective control from top to bottom to ensure that whatever mission the trustees have in mind is generally carried out, not subverted.

12. See the National Education Association Web site (www.nea.org) for data.

13. The unionization of graduate students is completely preposterous, but it has happened at a number of decent-quality schools. The AAUP asserts that it is consistent with academic freedom and quality education (see http://www.aaup.org/publications/academe/02mj/02mjAW.HTM), but we can think of few things that could be more destructive than giving students collective-bargaining rights.

14. Peter Drucker has noted that distance education is likely to become much more common owing both to the ability to provide such education at a reasonable price and to the need for continuing education over a working life (1998, 54). To get an idea of why some faculty members object so much to distance education, see Noble 2001.

15. For thoughtful comments on the matter, see Keffeler 1997.

16. A large number of studies are available on this point. For a good collection, see http://www.privatization.org. An original book in the area is Eggers and O'Leary 1995.

17. Faculty evaluations invariably produce high-minded protests against their use from some faculty (Trout 2000).

18. Legislatures bounce around on the issue of centralization of higher education, but there has been increased discussion of breaking up state-managed cartels (Schmidt 2001).

19. On the value of taxpayer subsidies to sports teams and stadiums, see the essays by Noll and Zimbalist (Noll and Zimbalist 1997).

References

AAUP at Work. 2002. *Academe* 88, no. 3 (May/June). Available at: http://www.aaup.org/publications/academe/02mj/02mjAW.HTM

AAUP v. Bloomfield College. 1974. 129 N.J.Super. 249.

Adamian v. Jacobsen. 1975. 523 F.2d 929 (5th Cir.).

Alchian, Armen, and Harold Demsetz. 1972. Production, Information Costs, and Economic Organization. *American Economic Review* 62: 777–95.

Altbach, Philip G. 2002. How Are Faculty Faring in Other Countries? In *The Questions of Tenure,* edited by Richard P. Chait, 160–81. Cambridge, Mass.: Harvard University Press.

Aman, Alfred C., and William T. Mayton. 2001. *Administrative Law.* 2d ed. St. Paul: West Group.

Beattie, Bruce. 1995. *Bureaucratic Behavior and Rent Seeking in the Ivory Tower (Including Agricultural Economics).* Benjamin H. Hibbard Memorial Lecture Series, Department of Agricultural Economics, University of Wisconsin, Madison.

Bennett, Michael. 1994. The Law That Worked. *Educational Record* 75, no. 4: 6–14.

Board of Regents of State Colleges v. Roth. 1972. 408 U.S. 564, 92 S.Ct. 2701 (Sup. Ct.).

Borsky v. Bd. of Regents. 1954. 147 U.S. 442.

Brimelow, Peter. 2003. *The Worm in the Apple.* New York: HarperCollins.

Brooks, Robert C. 1924. Tenure in Colleges and Universities. *School and Society* 19, no. 487 (April 26): 497–501.

Brubacher, John S., and Willis Rudy. 1958. *Higher Education in Transition: An American History: 1636–1956.* New York: Harper and Brothers.

Carroll, Linda L. 2000. Tenure and Academic Excellence. *Academe* 86, no. 3. Available at: http://www/aaup.org/publications/Academe/00mj/ML00Carr.htm

Chait, Richard P. 1995. The Future of Academic Tenure. *Priorities* (Association of Governing Boards). Spring: 1–12.

Chait, Richard P. 2002. Why Tenure, Why Now? In *The Questions of Tenure,* edited by Richard P. Chait, 6–31. Cambridge, Mass.: Harvard University Press.

Chandler, Alfred. 1962. *Strategy and Structure.* Cambridge, Mass.: MIT Press.

———. 1991. The Functions of the HQ Unit in the Multibusiness Firm. *Strategic Management Journal* 12 (winter): 31–50.

Committee on Academic Freedom and Tenure. 1932. Extracts from Annual Reports, 1923–1932. *Bulletin of the American Association of University Professors* (May): 333–47.

Committee on Academic Freedom. 1915. Report. *Bulletin of the American Association of University Professors* (December): 15–43

de Russy, Candace. 1996. In Defense of Activist Trusteeship. *Trusteeship* 4, no. 6: 6–10.

Developments in the Law: Academic Freedom. 1967–68. *Harvard Law Review* 81: 1045–159.

Drucker, Peter. 1993. *Post Capitalist Society.* New York: Harper Business.

———. 1995. Really Reinventing Government. *Atlantic Monthly* (February): 49–61.

———. 1998. The Next Information Revolution. *Forbes ASAP* (August 24): 47–58.

Eggers, William D., and John O'Leary. 1995. *Revolution at the Roots: Making Our Government Smaller, Better, and Closer to Home.* New York: Free Press.

Ferguson v. Thomas. 1970. 430 F.2d 852 (5th Cir.).

Frazier, Matt. 2003. Bill Would Make Texas Teachers' Dismissal Easier. *Fort Worth Star-Telegram,* February 21, 1A.

Garrett v. Matthews. 1979. 474 F.Supp. 594 (N.D. Ala.).

Gerber, Larry G. 2001. "Inextricably Linked": Shared Governance and Academic Freedom. *Academe* 87, no. 3. Available at: www.aaup.org/publications/Academe/01mj/mj01.gerb.htm.

Gilley, Wade, Kenneth Fulmer, and Sally Reithling. 1986. *Searching for Academic Excellence.* New York: Macmillan.

Gose, Ben. 1997a. Duke May Shift Grading System to Reward Students Who Take Challenging Classes. *Chronicle of Higher Education,* February 14, A47.

———. 1997b. Duke Rejects a Controversial Plan to Revise the Calculation of Grade-Point Averages. *Chronicle of Higher Education,* March 21, A53.

Greer, Darryl, and Paul Shelly. 1995. A State of Change: One Year Ago, New Jersey Reinvented Public Higher Education. *Trusteeship* 3, no. 4: 16–19, 35.

Hill, Charles, Michael Hitt, and Robert Hoskisson. 1992. Cooperative Versus Competitive Structures in Related and Unrelated Diversified Firms. *Organizational Science* 3, no. 4: 501–21.

Hofstadter, Richard, and Wilson Smith. 1961. *Higher Education in America.* Vol. 2. Chicago: University of Chicago Press.

Honan, William. 1994. New Pressures on the University. *New York Times,* January 9, sec. 4A, 16.

Joe Hill Takes on Joe College. 1996. *Business Week,* December 23, 60–61.

Johnson v. Bd. of Regents of U. Wisc. Sys. 1974. 377 F.Supp. 227 (W.D. Wisc.).

Joughlin, Louis, ed. 1969. *Academic Freedom and Tenure: A Handbook of the American Association of University Professors.* Madison: University of Wisconsin Press.

Kanter, Rosabeth. 1996. Can Giants Dance in Cyberspace? *Forbes ASAP* (December 2): S247–49.

Keffeler, Jean B. 1997. How Faculty Can Break the Impasse on Tenure. *Trusteeship* (November–December): 6–9.

Kerr, Clark. 1994. Expanding Access and Changing Missions. *Educational Record* 74, no. 4: 27–31.

Magner, Denise K. 1997. A Scholar Provides an Intellectual Framework for Plans to End or Revamp Tenure Systems. *Chronicle of Higher Education,* February 14, A10.

McAuliffe v. Mayor of New Bedford. 1892. 155 Mass. 216.

McCormick, Robert, and Roger Meiners. 1988. University Governance: A Property Rights Perspective. *Journal of Law and Economics* (October): 777–95.

McHugh, William F. 1973. Faculty Unionism. In *The Tenure Debate,* edited by Bardwell L. Smith, 244–61. San Francisco: Jossey-Bass.

McKee, Patrick W. 1980–81. Tenure by Default: The Nonformal Acquisition of Academic Tenure. *Journal of College and University Law.* 7: 31–56.

McLeod v. Beaty. 1998. 718 So.2d 682 (Sup. Ct., Ala.).

Meiners, Roger. 1995. The History of American Higher Education. In *The Academy in Crisis: The Political Economy of Higher Education,* edited by John Sommer, 21–43. New Brunswick, N.J.: Transaction, for The Independent Institute.

Meiners, Roger, and Roger Miller. 1996. *Gridlock in Government.* 2d ed. Indianapolis: State Policy Network.

Menard, A. P. 1975. May Tenure Rights of Faculty Be Bargained Away? *Journal of College and University Law* 2, no. 2: 256–68.

Merrifield, John. 2003. *School Choices: True and False*. Oakland: The Independent Institute.

Metzger, Walter P. 1973. Academic Tenure in America: A Historical Essay. In *Faculty Tenure: A Report and Recommendations by the Commission on Academic Tenure in Higher Education*, 93–159. New York: Jossey-Bass.

Minneapolis Star-Tribune. 1996. November 1, 3, and 7.

1940 Statement of Principles on Academic Freedom and Tenure. 1978. *Bulletin of the American Association of University Professors*: 108–12. Also available at: http://www.aaup.org/statements/Redbook/1940stat.htm.

Niskanen, William. 1971. *Bureaucracy and Representative Government*. Chicago: Aldine.

Noble, David. 2001. The Future of the Faculty in the Digital Diploma Mill. *Academe* 87, no. 5. Available at: http://www.aaup.org/publications/Academe/01SO/so01nob.htm.

Noll, Roger, and Andrew Zimbalist, eds. 1997. *Sports, Jobs, and Taxes*. Washington, D.C.: Brookings Institution.

Olson, Keith. 1994. The Astonishing Story. *Educational Record* 75, no. 4: 16–26.

O'Neal, Roger M. 1973. Tenure Under Attack. In *The Tenure Debate*, edited by Bardwell L. Smith, 57–88. San Francisco: Jossey-Bass.

Orzechowski, William. 1977. Economic Models of Bureaucracy. In *Budgets and Bureaucrats*, edited by Thomas Borcherding, 229–41. Durham, N.C.: Duke University Press.

Paarlberg, Don. 1992. The Land Grant College System in Transition. Choices 7, no. 3: 45.

Perry v. Sindermann. 1972. 408 U.S. 593, 92 S.Ct. 2694 (Sup. Ct.).

Peters, Tom. 1996. The Search for Excellence Continues. *Forbes ASAP* (December 2): S251–52.

Portland Press Herald (Maine). 1995. December 26.

Postel, Danny. 2003. "Vagina Monologues" Is First Canceled, Then Performed, at Xavier U. *Chronicle of Higher Education*, March 17, 18.

Rajan, Raghuram G. and Luigi Zingales. 2003. *Saving Capitalism from the Capitalists*. New York: Crown Business.

Report of the Committee of 1915. 1932. *Bulletin of the American Association of University Professors* (May): 378–91.

Rosovsky, Henry. 1987. Our Universities Are the World's Best. *The New Republic*, July 13 and 20: 13–14.

———. 1990. *The University: An Owner's Manual.* New York: Norton.

Sanderson, E. D. 1914. Definiteness of Appointment and Tenure. *Science* 39 (June 19): 890–96.

Scheuer v. Creighton University. 1977. 260 N.W.2d 595 (Sup. Ct., Neb.).

Schmidt, Peter. 2001. Weakening the Grip of Multicampus Boards. *Chronicle of Higher Education,* March 23: 24.

Selingo, Jeffrey. 2003. Massachusetts Governor Proposed Higher-Education Overhaul That Would Split UMass System. *Chronicle of Higher Education,* February 27: 1.

Seymour, Daniel. 1993. *On Q: Causing Quality in Higher Education.* New York: Oryx Press.

Shaw, B. N. 1971. *Academic Tenure in American Higher Education.* Chicago: Adams Press.

Siegfried, John, Malcolm Getz, and Kathryn Anderson. 1995. The Snail's Pace of Innovation in Higher Education. *Chronicle of Higher Education,* May 19: 24.

Smith, Adam. [1776] 1981. *An Inquiry into the Nature and Causes of the Wealth of Nations.* Indianapolis: Liberty Press.

Steinberg v. Elkins. 1979. 470 F.Supp. 1024 (D. Mary.).

Study of Tenure of University and College Teachers. 1932. *Bulletin of the American Association of University Professors* (April): 255–57.

Sykes, Charles J. 1988. *Profscam: Professors and the Demise of Higher Education.* Washington, D.C.: Regnery.

Tenure Is No Longer Untouchable at the University of Minnesota. 1997. *National Law Journal* (February 3): 1, 12.

Texas Higher Education Coordinating Board. 1994. *Administrative Expenditures in Texas Public Universities.* Austin.

Texas' Prescription for Doctor Glut. 1996. *Wall Street Journal* (Texas *Journal* edition), December 20, T4.

Trotman v. Bd. of Trustees of Lincoln Univ. 1980. 635 F.2d 216 (2d Cir.).

Trout, Paul. 2000. Flunking the Test: The Dismal Record of Student Evaluations. *Academe* 86, no. 4. Available at: http://www.aaup.org/publications /academe/00ja/JA00Trou.htm.

Trusteeship. 1996. *Two-Year Change in State Support for Higher Education* (November–December): 2.

U.S. News & World Report. 2003. *America's Best Colleges, 2004 Edition.*

Van Hise, Charles. 1910. The Appointment and Tenure of University Professors. *Journal of Proceedings and Addresses of the Association of American Universities* 12: 50–61.

Veblen, Thorstein. [1918] 1957. *The Higher Learning in America*. New York: Hill and Wang.

Wilson, Reginald. 1994. GI Bill Expands Access for African-Americans. *Educational Record* 75, no. 4: 32–39.

Wilson, Robin. 2002. Court Upholds Kansas State's Use of Post-Tenure Review to Dismiss Professor. *Chronicle of Higher Education*, November 29, A10.

Young, Jeffrey. 2003. Duke Professor Releases Data on Grade Inflation at 34 Colleges. *Chronicle of Higher Education*, January 30: 1.

Zimmer v. Spencer. 1973. 485 F.2d 176 (5th Cir.).

Index

Locators in **boldface** indicate tables.

About the Authors

RYAN C. AMACHER is Professor of Economics and Public Affairs and former President at the University of Texas at Arlington. He received his Ph.D. in economics from the University of Virginia, and he has served as Dean of the College of Commerce and Industry at Clemson University, Chairman of the Department of Economics at Arizona State University, Senior International Economist at the U.S. Department of the Treasury, Associate Professor of Economics at the University of Oklahoma, Economist at the General Electric TEMPO Center for Advanced Studies, and Consultant to the Federal Trade Commission. His books include *Economic Principles and Policy, Macroeconomic Principles and Policy, Microeconomic Principles and Policy, Core Concepts: Microeconomics, Federal Support of Higher Education, Challenges to a Liberal International Economic Order, The Economic Approach to Public Policy: Selected Readings, The Law of the Sea: U.S. Interests and Alternatives, Yugoslavia's Foreign Trade*; and *The Economics of the Military Draft*. He is the author of over 75 articles and reviews in scholarly journals. Professor Amacher is a member of the Board of Trustees of Ripon College, Texas Council on Economic Education, Institute for University Studies, and International Linguistics Center, and a past Board member of Texas Commerce Bank, South Carolina Council on Economic Education, and Arlington Chamber of Commerce.

ROGER E. MEINERS is professor of economics and law at the University of Texas at Arlington, research fellow at The

Independent Institute, and senior associate at PERC. Having received his Ph.D. in economics from Virginia Tech and J.D. from the University of Miami, he has served as director of the Center for Policy Studies at Clemson University, a faculty member at Texas A & M University and Emory University, director of the Atlanta Regional Office of the Federal Trade Commission, associate director of the Law and Economics Center at Emory University, and a member of the South Carolina Insurance Commission. He is the author or editor of numerous books including *Barriers to Corporate Growth* (with B. Baysinger and C. Zeithami), *Economic Consequences of Liability Rules* (with B. Yandle), *Federal Support of Higher Education* (with R. Amacher), *Government v. the Environment* (with D. Leal), *Managing in the Legal Environment* (with A. Ringleb and F. Edwards), *Taking the Environment Seriously* (with B. Yandle), *Victim Compensation*, and The Independent Institute books *Cutting Green Tape* (with R. Stroup) and *Regulation and the Reagan Era* (with B. Yandle).

INDEPENDENT INSTITUTE STUDIES IN POLITICAL ECONOMY

For further information or to request a catalog of publications, please contact:
THE INDEPENDENT INSTITUTE
100 Swan Way, Oakland, California 94621-1428, U.S.A. • Website: www.independent.org
Telephone: 510-632-1366 • Fax: 510-568-6040 • Email: info@independent.org